BEAT THAT!
— COOKBOOK —

Other cookbooks by Ann Hodgman

Beat This! Cookbook

BEAT THAT!
— COOKBOOK —

Ann Hodgman

Illustrations by Robin Zingone

CHAPTERS PUBLISHING, LTD., SHELBURNE, VERMONT 05482

Published by
Chapters Publishing Ltd.
2031 Shelburne Road
Shelburne, Vermont 05482

Mustard-Glazed Flank Steak from **For Goodness Taste** by the Junior League of Rochester, New York. Reprinted by permission of the Junior League of Rochester. All rights reserved.

Library of Congress Cataloging-in-Publication Data

Hodgman, Ann.
Beat That! cookbook / by Ann Hodgman ; illustrations by Robin Zingone.
    p.   cm.
The Very, Very Best Recipe for Apple Crisp, Baked Beans, Cheese Soufflé, English Muffin Bread, Flank Steak, Hot Chocolate, Key Lime Pie, Lasagna, Macaroni and Cheese, Party Shrimp, Roast Beef, Smoked Salmon Spirals, Orange Buttermilk Sherbet, Waffles and over 100 other recipes to make you levitate with joy.
    Includes index.
    ISBN 1-881527-92-1
    1. Cookery, American. I. Title.
    TX715.H72328 1995
    641.5973—dc20   95-9090

Trade distribution in Canada by
Firefly Books Ltd.
250 Sparks Avenue, Willowdale, Ontario
Canada M2H 2S4

Trade distribution in the U.S. by
Firefly Books (U.S.) Inc.
P.O. Box 1338, Ellicott Station
Buffalo, NY 14205

Printed and bound in Canada by
Best Book Manufacturers, Inc.
Louiseville, Quebec

Cover illustration by Robin Zingone
Cover design by Susan McClellan
Inside design by Eugenie Seidenberg Delaney

For Keanu Reeves

Acknowledgments

I FEEL FUNNY about having any acknowledgments in my slim volumes. I don't want to be one of those authors who thanks her college professors "for all they taught me about literature" when she publishes her first Little Golden Book. Still, lots of people helped me with this little golden book, and I want to mention them whether it's pretentious or not.

Readers were especially helpful. In *Beat This!*, I issued The Ann Hodgman Challenge. "Are your recipes better than these?" I asked. "I can't believe it. But if you think your potato salad will make me lie down and cry with shame, send it in. . . . If I get enough recipes together, I'll be able to do another cookbook."

It was perfect that the very first recipe I received *was* for potato salad, and it *did* make me lie down and cry with shame. Well, not really, but it was better than either of my two recipes. (See page 117 if you want to try it.)

In addition to submitting their own recipes, many readers also suggested "bests" I'd omitted from *Beat This! Cookbook*. Crackers, hot chocolate, pumpkin pie and roast beef were among these. My brother-in-law suggested homemade popcorn, too, but these days I can't seem to get beyond the microwaveable kind. Anyone out there know how to make the best "real" popcorn?

My friends and relatives also came marching out of the woodwork with various other delicious recipes to thrust into my hands. I'm indebted to everyone whose recipes or suggestions have so enriched these pages. If they have enriched these pages, I mean; if the book turns out to be a flop, I'm going to say it's everyone else's fault.

I'm indebted as well to my wonderful, darling agent, Susan Cohen. This book and its predecessor would never have been written without her encouragement; indeed, there was a long, long time when she was the only person who thought my idea was a good one.

My editors Rux Martin and Barry Estabrook are equally wonderful and darling, and Rux was more patient with my dilatoriness than you would ever believe. Lionel Koffler thought of this book's title, thank God.

The people at Television Food Network allowed me to take up valuable space both on the air and in their offices. Michael Ackerman, Pantry proprietor, was, as always, a great culinary source, and I'm not saying that just because he remembers that I used to write Nancy Drew mysteries. Ann Burton, dean of the Swiss Hospitality Institute Cesar Ritz, generously offered the school as a resource. Sandra Daniels, director of the Silo Cooking School, has been very helpful as well. Besides, it *can't* be a coincidence that we met on the day that our pet turtles were both at the vet's office having I.V. drips.

Sebiha Ceric, a great friend and an unparalleled cook, introduced me to Bosnian cuisine, especially burek. My mother, Joanna Hodgman, was a devoted and sensitive proofreader, text-tweaker and recipe-tester.

In various ways, Leah Chapin, Bob Ficks, Lisa Diamond, Mark Scholtz and Amy Tompkins made order out of chaos, and I wouldn't dream of giving a party without Lois Kramer and Linda McGarr to steer me straight. Matt Oseroff had nothing to do with this book, but I still wish I could have thanked him for various things.

Moxie is a terrible, stupid dog, but I love her anyway.

The birds and the prairie dog kept me company in the kitchen when I had late-night recipe testing to do. So did Nutcracker, an orphaned sugar glider who had to be hand-raised during the last weeks that I was finishing this book. And of course there wouldn't be any point to *anything* without David, Laura and John.

Contents

Introduction 10

Hors d'Oeuvres and Appetizers 12

Breads and Breakfast Foods 32

Soups and Sandwiches 60

Main Dishes 70

Vegetables and Side Dishes 104

Sauces and Chutneys 136

Desserts 146

Hot Chocolate, Iced Tea and Flubber 190

Leftovers 196

Index 203

Introduction

"Butter is my boyfriend," my goddaughter Sarah announced when she was four years old. It seems as good a theme for this book as any. The butter in *Beat This! Cookbook* made a lot of people mad, and they'll be just as mad to see that I haven't mended my ways in *this* cookbook. Let me deal with this first of all.

It's not that *Beat This!* didn't make people mad for other reasons. People get touchy when you tell them that your recipe for potato salad is better than their aunt's. People don't like hearing that the best barbecue sauce available has to be bought, not made. People faint dead away when you belittle Katharine Hepburn's brownies. "Ann Hodgman doesn't even sound like a nice person," someone told a friend of mine after reading *Beat This!*

But nothing made people madder than the butter in *Beat This!* "Can't you just make your next cookbook a little healthier this time around?" they kept asking. Well, no! I can't! I don't even want to!

My goal here is to give you the best recipes for the old standards people claim *they* have the best recipes for (but I really do). The best, I said—not the lowest in fat. I agree that low-fat food is important; it just doesn't have a place in this particular book. Besides, I'm not the boss of you. No one's forcing you to use my recipes. If you want a low-fat cookbook, go buy one. There were quite a few good ones in the stores the last time I looked. But if you want a cookbook with the best pancakes you'll ever make—or the best macaroni and cheese, or the best hot chocolate, or Key lime pie or popovers—stick around.

After all, when's the last time you heard someone brag, "My grandmother makes the healthiest stuffed potatoes you ever saw"? I bet that when your grandmother knows you're coming over, she pulls out the best recipe for stuffed potatoes she has, not the one that's lowest in fat. Of course she never will have been able to pull out the best recipe for stuffed potatoes until she reads this book, but that's beside the point. The point is that the food you want people to know you for—the food you want to *brag* about—is the food that tastes best.

I'm not saying you need to use the best recipes every minute of every day. Another thing I get asked a lot is, "Do you really eat that way all the time?" Of course I don't. I have two children, and I'd like them to reach adulthood with their arteries intact. Moreover, my husband and I, though we're both *enchanting* people, never seem to err on the thin side. We can't sit around pouring heavy cream down our throats any more than you can. We have to take the skin off our chicken just like everyone else.

But when we have people over, or we have to take a dish to a potluck, or it's a holiday, or when some other special occasion is brewing and we want ceremonial food instead of plain old everyday food, then I try to make the best food I can. If that bothers you, accept my deepest apologies.

There. I've apologized. I can't do any more than that. Now let's move on. Oh! Wait, there's one more thing.

Some readers have written in to complain about my occasionally using convenience foods. For the most part, I agree that convenience foods are gross and embarrassing and that usually they taste worse than regular foods. On the other hand, once in awhile they can be delicious, and in those cases, it would be mean of me not to tell you about them—even though it does sully whatever is left of my reputation.

Besides, I always remember what a friend of mine once said. "If I can't find the ingredients at Stop & Shop, I won't make the recipe at all. I get too discouraged." I want people like her to use this book too.

However, I haven't bowed to the many people who prefer fake whipped cream to real—which is, apparently, most of the American population. (In blind taste tests, fake whipped cream consistently outperforms real.) No matter how many of

them there are, they're wrong.

Beat That! is organized more conventionally than *Beat This!* was. This time around, I've divided the recipes into groups rather than presenting them alphabetically. The alphabetical approach drove many readers crazy, especially—for some reason—men. It only seemed necessary at the time because I was afraid everyone would notice the book's disproportionate percentage of desserts. There are still too many desserts in *this* book, but at least I've included a few more meats and vegetables. At least, I think I have. I haven't really counted.

Hors d'Oeuvres and Appetizers

THEY'RE NOT REALLY WELL NAMED. Rather than being "outside of work," they *are* work, and lots of it. Thank God filo is finally going out of style; buttering all those leaves of dough used to take up years of my life.

But hors d'oeuvres are worth all the work. Many years ago, my husband gave me a tiny plastic Yoda figure dressed in a tiny fuzzy robe. "Oh, he's adorable!" a friend of mine cooed. "He's so *bite-sized!*" (She was talking about the Yoda.) Bite-sizedness—isn't that the best thing about an hors d'oeuvre? So much taste packed into such a little space.

Oh, there's no way I can do justice to hors d'oeuvres, in this or any other cookbook. I love all of them, even cocktail franks in grape jelly sauce. I'd much rather spoil my appetite on appetizers than keep myself hungry for the meal.

A couple of years ago, I decided that serving Christmas dinner on Christmas Day was too hard for all of us. I always had to start cooking the minute the presents were opened, and for the rest of the day, my family would seem like impediments to getting dinner done on time rather than dear, beloved relatives who only needed a couple of minutes' help setting up their dollhouse.

So I switched our formal dinner to December 26 instead, and on the "real" Christmas, I started serving a dinner of hors-d'oeuvres, finger desserts and champagne. It was so much more fun than a regular meal that I'm starting to wonder if perhaps December 26 should become our once-a-year occasion for eating a real dinner. The rest of the time, we may stick to bite-sized.

Recipes

Seven-Layer Dip 14

Crocked Shrimp 16

Lumpia (Philippine Egg Rolls) 18

God's Granola 21

Many-Splendored Guacamole 24

Spiced Vanilla Pecans 25

Pepper-Parmesan Cocktail Shortbread 26

Smoked Salmon Spirals 27

Party Shrimp 28

Sarah's Tomato Sandwiches 30

Seven-Layer Dip

This, the only dip I bother with besides Crocked Shrimp (page 16), is *rawther* a lot of work. But I don't mind, because I *like* making my friends happy, and my friends like Seven-Layer Dip so much that they would eat it with ladles if they could. I usually make the guacamole and bean dips the day before I assemble what you might call the "total dip." The recipe makes a ton.

I don't use my Many-Splendored Guacamole (page 24) for this recipe; it would only get lost in all the dip's *other* splendors. I just make regular guacamole.

Bean Layer

1	16-ounce can kidney or pinto beans, drained and rinsed
2	tablespoons finely chopped, seeded jalapeño peppers, or to taste
1	tablespoon cider vinegar
1	teaspoon chili powder
½	teaspoon ground cumin
1	tablespoon minced fresh parsley
	Salt to taste

Guacamole Layer

3	ripe avocados, halved, peeled and pitted
1	small red onion, minced
2	scallions, chopped fine
2	large garlic cloves, chopped fine
2	tablespoons fresh cilantro, chopped fine
¼	cup fresh lime juice, or to taste
2	teaspoons ground cumin
1	teaspoon freshly ground pepper
	Salt to taste

3 large tomatoes, deglopped and chopped *fine*
¾ cup salsa, well drained (you decide how hot you want it to be)
1 pint sour cream
2 cups grated extra-sharp Cheddar
Many, many tortilla chips as an accompaniment

Bean layer: In a medium bowl, mash everything together until relatively smooth.

Guacamole layer: Ditto. If you're making the guacamole ahead of time, cover it very tightly with plastic wrap. Don't bother burying an avocado pit inside the bowl to keep the guacamole green; it won't work. Only keeping guacamole tart (with lime juice) and airtight (with plastic wrap) preserves its color—but it's still not going to be grass-green after 24 hours. No one will notice.

Other things: In a large, straight-sided baking dish or other serving module, spread the bean dip across the bottom. Spread half of the chopped tomatoes over the bean dip. Spread the guacamole over the chopped tomatoes. Spread the drained salsa over the guacamole; the sour cream over the salsa; the other half of the tomatoes over the sour cream; and the grated Cheddar—yes—over the tomatoes. You could sprinkle some chopped black olives over the cheese for color, but I don't much like olives. Of course, the olives would enable you to call this *Eight-*Layer Dip.

Serve with lots of tortilla chips, and stand out of the way as people charge toward you.

Makes enough for a large party—say, 20 or more people. I once made this amount at a cocktail party for 150, and we still had some left over. But there was an awful lot of other food at that party. I think some of it may still be in our freezer.

> **"My friends would eat this dip with ladles if they could."**

Crocked Shrimp

CROCKED SHRIMP is just about the only dip-type recipe I can bring myself to make. It stands loftily upon the shoulders of all the other dips, gazing out into the sunset or whatever.

Returning to earth now: You have to start this two days ahead. Don't you *love* starting recipes a few days ahead? It makes me so happy to think of ingredients gently melding and marrying as the hours pass.

This recipe is from my sister's sister-in-law, Mimi DiMatteo.

First Day

2	cups water
1	cup dry white wine
2	lemons, sliced
3	large garlic cloves, chopped
1	tablespoon whole black peppercorns
1	tablespoon yellow mustard seeds
1½	pounds raw medium shrimp, unpeeled

Second Day

8	ounces Philadelphia cream cheese, softened
3	flat anchovy fillets, rinsed (don't worry if you don't like anchovies; their flavor won't stick out)
¼	cup (½ stick) unsalted butter, softened
1	tablespoon fresh lemon juice, or to taste
1	tablespoon Dijon mustard
2	small scallions, minced (include some of the green)
	Salt and freshly ground pepper to taste
	Water crackers and thin-sliced cucumbers for serving

First day: Combine everything except the shrimp in a medium nonreactive saucepan over high heat. Bring the liquid to a boil; then cover it partway and let it boil for 10 minutes. Reduce heat to medium-low, stir in the shrimp (still in their shells) and simmer for 3 minutes. Let the shrimp cool in the liquid and then chill them, covered, overnight.

Second day: Drain and peel the shrimp. In a food processor, combine the cream cheese, anchovies, butter, lemon juice and Dijon mustard. Process until smooth. Drop in the shrimp and use on-off pulses to chop it finely. Leaving a bit of shrimpy texture is fine.

Transfer the mixture to a large bowl, stir in the scallions and season with the salt and pepper. Cover the bowl tightly with plastic wrap and chill it overnight.

Let the shrimp sit for 1 hour at room temperature before serving it with water crackers and thin-sliced cucumbers.

Serves 10.

Lumpia (Philippine Egg Rolls)

THE RECIPE FOR THESE MARVELS comes from the most wonderful plastic surgeon in the world, Teresita Mascardo. What makes Lumpia so great is their slimness as well as their filling. In Terry's skilled hands, they're pencil-thin. They're more cumbersome when you and I make them, but that's because we're not plastic surgeons.

As befits a surgeon's recipe, Lumpia are painstaking and time-consuming. (You wouldn't believe what teensy, perfect cubes Terry cuts her vegetables into.) You need to turn these egg rolls into an occasion of their own. The best thing to do is to invite a bunch of friends over to sit around the kitchen for a couple of hours, making the egg rolls and eating them as soon as they're cooked. Ideally, you should be sitting around Terry's kitchen making them with her. Then you can stroll around her property and see her pool house.

The egg rolls are really best served right away, but my husband inhaled them straight from the refrigerator the next day, including the ones I'd earmarked for myself.

Egg Rolls

½	pound ground pork
½	pound raw shrimp, chopped very fine
4	medium carrots, chopped fine
1	large onion, chopped fine
4-6	large scallions, chopped fine (as much of the green part as possible)
1	small can water chestnuts, chopped fine ("Terry-chopped," my recipe says)
4	large eggs
¼	cup soy sauce, or more to taste
2	teaspoons freshly ground pepper
2	teaspoons Accent (optional)
1	pound egg roll wrappers

Corn oil for deep-frying

**Sauce for Party Shrimp (page 29), or
Terry's Dipping Sauce (page 20)**

Egg rolls: In a large bowl, mix together everything with a spoon except the egg roll wrappers and oil. Stir gently, trying to keep the ingredients as unmashed as possible. Cook a small amount of the filling in a small skillet or microwave so that you can check the seasonings. Add more pepper, soy sauce and Accént if you want. Chill the filling for 1 hour, or until firm.

Slice each egg roll wrapper in half lengthwise. In a deep-fryer or deep, heavy pot, pour in the corn oil to a 3-inch depth. Heat the oil until a dropped-in bread cube sizzles instantly. (If you're using a frying thermometer, the oil should be about 360 degrees F.) Fill a small bowl with water and keep it near your work surface.

To make the egg rolls, spread 1 tablespoon of filling evenly along the long top edge of each halved wrapper, leaving a half-inch border.

Fold the border over the line of filling. With your forefinger, paint a line of water along the folded-over border. Roll up the wrapper as tightly as you can, sealing it with another line of water applied with your finger. Using water as a sealant will keep the rolls from unwrapping.

With a sharp knife, cut each thin, thin egg roll into thirds—3 *small*, thin egg rolls. Using a slotted spoon, slip the egg rolls a few at a time into the hot oil and fry them, turning them often, until they're brown and crispy. Drain and serve them immediately.

You don't have to serve these with a sauce, but I myself like gilding lilies. Terry uses a sweet and sour tomato-based sauce for her egg rolls. I use my Party Shrimp sauce. Another woman I know mixes equal parts of soy sauce and white vinegar, adding minced fresh ginger and scallions to taste. All are good.

Makes 120 tiny egg rolls.

(continued)

"My husband inhaled these straight from the refrigerator."

Terry's Dipping Sauce

TERRY'S SAUCE USES A VINEGAR that has red peppers floating in it. I was scared when I first saw this; I thought the peppers were gold-fish.

1   teaspoon corn oil
3   tablespoons ketchup
¼   cup chicken broth
¼   cup white, cider or pepper-flavored vinegar
¼   cup sugar
1   tablespoon cornstarch
    Salt, freshly ground pepper and Tabasco to taste
    Minced scallions to taste (optional)

In a small skillet over medium heat, heat the corn oil. Add the ketchup and heat it until it begins to separate. (Be forewarned that the mixture will spatter as it heats.) Add the remaining ingredients and heat, whisking constantly, until the sauce is as thick as pudding. This will keep it from dripping off onto your shirt when you dip the egg rolls in it. Off the heat, stir in the optional scallions. Transfer to a small bowl.

Makes 1 scant cup.

"When I first saw this, I thought the peppers were goldfish."

God's Granola

(also known as Asian Ambrosia)

(also known as Posy's Cheewrah)

(ALSO known as St. John's Trail Mix)

CHEEWRAH IS A SORT OF INDIAN COCKTAIL MIX, and what a horri-fyingly delicious recipe this is. By horrifying, I mean that you start out by taking a pinch of nuts with your fingers and then find yourself pouring a big bowl of it and eating it with a spoon. After about half an hour, you'd like to stop, but you can't. When your lips are blistered and itchy from salt and spices, and all you want to do is drink quarts of water, you vow that you'll never eat it again. Then, the next day, you take another tiny pinch just to see if it's still as good as you thought, and you repeat the entire process. You continue until you topple over.

To reduce this risk, serve this granola only to large gatherings. That way no one gets hurt. Posy Benedict and I sold this at a church bazaar along with Posy's Chutney (page 141).

Making God's Granola involves a lot of steps as well as a rather rarefied list of ingredients. But it's not as complicated as it looks. If you're the kind of person who isn't irritated by this kind of recipe, I beg you to try it.

1	teaspoon salt
1	teaspoon ground cinnamon
1	teaspoon cayenne, or less to taste
½	teaspoon freshly ground pepper
¼	teaspoon ground cloves
	About 2 cups corn oil for frying, plus 1½ tablespoons for sautéing
½	cup dried chick-peas (available at Indian stores, some specialty shops and most health-food stores)
¼	cup *each* golden raisins, dark raisins and dried cherries
1	cup raw cashews
1	cup raw peanuts, without those gross papery skins

1 teaspoon black mustard seeds (available at Indian stores, some specialty shops and some health-food stores)

1 pinch ground asafetida (available at Indian stores, some specialty shops and some health-food stores— this is optional, but well worth it)

3 tablespoons sesame seeds

¼ teaspoon ground turmeric

3 cups Rice Krispies

2 teaspoons sugar

1½ teaspoons ground *amchoor* (dried, powdered mango, available at Indian stores) or finely chopped dried mango (available at health food stores), optional

In a small bowl, stir together the salt, cinnamon, cayenne, pepper and cloves. Put them somewhere that you won't forget about them.

> "What a horrifyingly delicious recipe this is."

Line 2 cookie sheets with several thicknesses of paper towel. Preheat the oven to 350 degrees F. Have a sieve at the ready.

O-*kay*. It's time to deep-fry the dried chick-peas. In a wok, deep skillet or other deep-frying vessel, pour enough corn oil to reach a depth of 1 inch. Heat until the oil is hot enough to make a dropped-in chick-pea sizzle immediately. Then put the chick-peas into a sieve and set the sieve carefully into the oil. Cook until the chick-peas are sizzling all over. Drain them on half of the paper-towel-lined cookie sheet.

Now fry 2 tablespoons of the golden raisins, 2 tablespoons of the dark raisins and 2 tablespoons of the dried cherries in the same way. You want to cook them until they puff up like little spheres—a fun thing to watch. Drain the first sieveful on part of the first cookie sheet and repeat the process with the remaining 2 tablespoons of each of the dried fruits.

Put the cashews and peanuts on a large baking pan or rimmed cookie sheet. Take out 2 tablespoons of the "raisin oil" and stir into the nuts. Bake the nuts for 10 to 12 minutes, stirring frequently, until they are golden and cooked through. Drain them on the second lined cookie sheet. You're almost done, I promise.

In a small skillet, over low heat, heat the remaining 1½ tablespoons oil. When it's hot, put in the mustard seeds and the optional asafetida. Stir these constantly for a few seconds, until the seeds begin to pop. Then add the sesame seeds and stir *them* constantly until they're golden brown. Add the turmeric, stir for 3 seconds and take the skillet off the heat.

In a large bowl, stir together the fried spices and their oil, the ingredients on the cookie sheets, the Rice Krispies, the dried spices from the beginning of this recipe long, long ago, the sugar and optional *amchoor* or dried mango. Toss everything together well. Cool the granola thoroughly, give it a final toss and store it airtight at room temperature.

Makes about 6 cups.

Many-Splendored Guacamole

I THOUGHT THE GUACAMOLE in *Beat This!* was about as good as guacamole gets until my friend Laura Lloyd told me about *her* friend Sarah Becker's guacamole. "I was fully levitated when I tasted it," Laura said. Well! Naturally I couldn't deny myself and others the same chance. I hate to admit it, but Sarah's guacamole was way better than mine. You absolutely have to try it. It has a billion ingredients, but that's because it's so perfectly fine-tuned that it *needs* lots of ingredients. I have changed two things that were mandatory in the original. I don't like black olives, and I think jicama is the water chestnut of the crudité world: all texture, no flavor. But you'll levitate whether or not you put in the jicama or, for that matter, olives. If you can't find chorizo—a dry, spicy sausage— you can substitute kielbasa or andouille. Or you can leave out the chorizo.

4	ripe avocados, preferably Hass
2	tablespoons fresh lemon juice
2	scallions, chopped (include as much green as possible)
2	large garlic cloves, minced
2	jalapeños, seeded and minced
1	medium tomato, deglopped and chopped
2	tablespoons grated and peeled jicama (optional)
1	tablespoon sour cream
1	tablespoon Worcestershire sauce
1	tablespoon olive oil
1	tablespoon white-wine vinegar
2	teaspoons ground cumin
2	teaspoons chili powder
¼	cup "medium" salsa
¼	cup grated Monterey Jack
¼	cup minced chorizo sausage
2	tablespoons tequila
2	tablespoons minced fresh cilantro
1	teaspoon salt

In a medium bowl, mash the avocados. Stir in the other ingredients in order. Wrap the guacamole tightly in plastic wrap if you're not serving it right away.

Makes 5½ cups.

Spiced Vanilla Pecans

TRULY THE LAST WORD IN SPICED NUTS: Look no farther. This recipe comes from my sister-in-law Mimi Owen, who says that no matter how many batches she makes for a party, it's never enough. I find that more people say, "You *made* these?" than they do for almost anything else I make. (Unless you plan to start before dawn, the first part of this recipe must be done a day ahead.)

1	pound whole pecan halves
6	cups water
½	cup superfine sugar (see page 201)
3	tablespoons unsalted butter, melted
1	tablespoon light corn syrup
1	tablespoon vanilla extract
¼	teaspoon salt
¼	teaspoon ground coriander
¼	teaspoon ground cinnamon
¼	teaspoon freshly grated nutmeg
¼	teaspoon ground allspice
⅛	teaspoon freshly ground pepper

In a large saucepan, boil the pecans in the water for 1 minute. Drain well. While they're still hot, toss them in a large bowl with the sugar, melted butter, corn syrup and vanilla extract. Mix well and let the nuts sit, covered, for at least 12 hours, up to 24.

Preheat the oven to 325 degrees F. Put the nuts on a rimmed cookie sheet. Bake them for 30 minutes, stirring them every 5 minutes. The nuts should be well browned—though I realize they start out brown, so what you're looking for is a *darker* brown—and crisp-looking. Of course they won't really be crisp until they're cool. Meanwhile, combine all the spices in a large bowl. The instant the nuts are done, add them to the spices and toss until they're well coated.

Pat the nuts back down on the cookie sheet in a single layer, so that they can cool without clumping. Cool them thoroughly and store airtight.

Makes 1 pound.

Pepper-Parmesan Cocktail Shortbread

THIS RECIPE IS NOT ONLY VERY GOOD, it's very easy. Sure, grinding all that pepper is a little tiresome, but you can just think of it as finger exercise. And speaking of pepper, don't omit the salt sprinkled on top of the shortbread before baking. For some reason that I'd probably have to be a biochemist to understand, it makes a huge difference.

2 cups all-purpose flour
5 ounces Parmesan, cut into small chunks
1 tablespoon or more freshly ground pepper
1 "shake" of cayenne
1 cup (2 sticks) unsalted butter, chilled and cut into 16 slices
Salt for sprinkling on top of the shortbread

Preheat the oven to 325 degrees F.

In a food processor, process the flour and the Parmesan until the mixture resembles cornmeal. Add the pepper and cayenne and process for a few more seconds.

Scatter the butter slices over the flour mixture and process with on-off pulses until the mixture forms a ball. Press it into a 9-inch pie pan. With a fork, pierce the dough all over, right down to the pan. Lightly sprinkle salt all over the dough.

Bake the shortbread for 45 minutes, or until it's a rich golden brown. (Sweet shortbread isn't supposed to brown, but it's okay for this one to.) Let the pan cool on a rack for 10 minutes. With a sharp knife, cut the shortbread into 16 to 20 thin slices.

Allow the shortbread to finish cooling completely before you remove it from the pan. I take it out by upending the pie pan onto a cookie sheet so that the shortbread slides out upside down. Then I re-upend the shortbread onto a serving plate. If I'm really feeling fancy, I fan out the slices and place a bit of parsley or a few peppercorns between each slice.

Makes 16 to 20 shortbread wedges.

Smoked Salmon Spirals

As a rule, I think smoked salmon should be left sternly alone. I don't mean alone in the sense of not being eaten, because I think everyone, especially me and my husband, should eat lots of it; I mean that it shouldn't be tinkered with. It's too good to mess up. I especially don't think smoked salmon should ever be heated—in pasta, for example—because that always turns it into *canned* salmon.

But then we come to this recipe—an adaptation of a Sarah Leah Chase creation—which is too good not to make. And maybe we could say it's really a *streamlined* way of serving smoked salmon, in that it combines all the things that taste best with smoked salmon in one easy mouthful. Whenever I serve these spirals, people bolt them down without even chewing, like seals catching fish.

1	pound Philadelphia cream cheese, softened
1	tablespoon *each* fresh lemon juice and grated lemon rind
3	scallions, minced (include as much green as possible)
3	tablespoons minced fresh dill, plus more for garnish
2	teaspoons Hungarian sweet paprika
8	large flour tortillas, 10 to 12 inches in diameter
2	tablespoons small capers, drained
1	pound smoked salmon, thinly sliced

Beat together the cream cheese, lemon juice and rind, scallions, dill and paprika. When these ingredients are well mixed, stir in the capers.

Spread each tortilla with one-eighth of the cream-cheese mixture, leaving a ¼-inch margin. Cover the cream cheese with slices of salmon.

Roll up the tortillas tightly, pressing down hard as you roll. Wrap each rolled tortilla in plastic wrap like a Tootsie Roll. Chill at least 3 hours, not longer than 12.

To serve, slice the rolls ½ inch thick. All the uneven ends are for you, of course. Arrange the slices on a serving dish and garnish each with a tiny dill sprig.

Makes about 60 spirals, because you'll want to eat the "end" ones so as to avoid serving uneven-looking slices.

> "People bolt these down without chewing, like seals catching fish."

Party Shrimp

SOMETIMES I SERVE SHRIMP AT PARTIES. It's a big cliché, I know. *Bring out the shrimp and the pigs in blankets and the rumaki!* But what can you do? People have to have shrimp at parties. People rush nice Lois and Linda, who are helping you at the party, and grab fistfuls of shrimp off their trays. People *hoard* shrimp at parties, even the flabbiest, most-reeking-of-the-freezer shrimp. Give in gracefully, I say, and serve them the best shrimp you can.

One secret, which I discovered in *Cook's Magazine*, is brining the shrimp before you cook it. This so improves the taste and texture that *Cook's* claims you can even use it to disguise those flabby freezer shrimp. I haven't had the nerve to try that, but fortunately even good shrimp can be improved by brining it beforehand. A second secret is adding sesame oil to the water in which you poach the shrimp. And a third is making a sauce that looks exactly like cocktail sauce but tastes nothing like it.

At the last party I gave—I don't want to sound as though I give parties all the time; I hardly ever do—the shrimp never got out to the party. People ate it all up while it was still out in the kitchen waiting to be served. For this reason, I suggest buying way more shrimp than you think you'll need. I've never had any leftovers, and I *want* some.

Brine Solution

5	pounds large or jumbo shrimp, unpeeled
3	*cups* kosher salt
3	cups boiling water
6	cups cold water

Poaching Water

10	cups water
2	lemons, cut into chunks
1	large onion, cut into chunks
2	bay leaves
1	tablespoon whole black peppercorns
1	tablespoon Asian sesame oil

Sauce
1½	cups canned tomato puree
1	tablespoon light brown sugar
1	large garlic clove, crushed
¼	cup fresh lime juice
1	teaspoon grated lime rind
¼	teaspoon cayenne, or to taste
1	tablespoon cornstarch, dissolved in 1 tablespoon water
3	tablespoons minced fresh cilantro
	Salt to taste

Brine solution: Peel the shrimp and devein them, if you care about the vein. I don't, unless it's filled with black gunk. In a large nonreactive pot, add the salt to the boiling water. Stir until you've dissolved as much salt as possible; then add the cold water and stir until you've dissolved *all* the salt. If it's a very hot day, part of the cold water may be replaced with ice cubes. Put the shrimp into the water and let stand for 45 minutes—*no longer*. Drain and rinse well under cold running water.

Poaching water: Rinse out the pot. Into it, place the poaching ingredients. Bring the liquid to a boil and boil it hard for 5 minutes. Stir in the shrimp and lower the heat so the shrimp are just simmering gently. Cook the shrimp for 3 to 5 minutes, or until they are pink and curled. Drain them again, dry them with paper towels if need be, and put them into the fridge to get nice and cold.

The sauce: In a medium nonreactive saucepan, stir together the tomato puree, brown sugar, garlic, lime juice and rind and cayenne. Bring these ingredients to a boil over medium heat, stirring frequently. When they're boiling, stir in the cornstarch-water mixture. Stirring constantly, cook the sauce until it has thickened slightly. (Remember that it thickens more once it's cooled.) Take the sauce off the heat and cool it completely. Stir in the cilantro. Cover and chill the sauce until you're ready for it.

Serve as for shrimp cocktail. An antic voice inside me wants to add, ". . . and let the fun begin!" but I won't let it.

Serves 20, and I bet you *still* won't have leftovers.

"Serving shrimp at parties is a big cliché, I know."

Sarah's Tomato Sandwiches

BEFORE SHE EMBARKED on a church career, Sarah Gaede was a caterer. This hors d'oeuvre recipe was one of her most popular. People used to follow the tray around, snatching sandwiches off it. This is an exacting recipe, but utterly worthwhile.

Sandwiches: Take a 2½-to-3-inch round biscuit cutter to the store with you when you buy your tomatoes. It is important to have tomatoes the same size as the cutter or slightly smaller.

Spicy Mayonnaise

1	small onion
1	large egg
2	large egg yolks
1	tablespoon white-wine vinegar
1	tablespoon fresh lemon juice
1	teaspoon salt
1	teaspoon cayenne
1	teaspoon celery seed
2	cups corn oil

Sandwiches

2	loaves Pepperidge Farm extra-thin white bread
2	loaves Pepperidge Farm extra-thin whole-wheat bread
12	small ripe tomatoes
12	ounces bacon

Spicy mayonnaise: In a food processor, chop the onion fine. Add the remaining ingredients, except for the oil, and process for 1 minute. With the machine running, pour in the oil slowly through the feed tube. Taste the mayonnaise for seasoning and adjust if necessary. Scrape into a small bowl, cover and refrigerate immediately. This is best made 24 hours ahead.

Sandwiches: With the cutter, cut rounds from the bread and store them in an airtight container at room temperature. (This may be done 1 day ahead.) Cook the bacon until very crisp, 10 to 12 minutes (Sarah bakes it in the oven at 375 degrees F). Drain it well on paper towels and crumble it.

Core and slice each tomato into 5 slices and push out the gooshy parts with your fingers. Drain the slices on a rack over a baking sheet.

Assembling the sandwiches: Line a baking sheet with wax paper. Spread the white bread rounds with the spicy mayonnaise and place them on the baking sheet. Place a tomato slice on each bread round.

Sprinkle each round with crumbled bacon.

Spread the whole-wheat bread rounds with more mayonnaise and place them, mayonnaise side down, on top of the other rounds. You can layer the sandwiches no more than 3 deep, with wax paper or plastic wrap between layers. Cover the sandwiches tightly with plastic wrap and refrigerate them until serving.

Makes about 60 hors d'oeuvres.

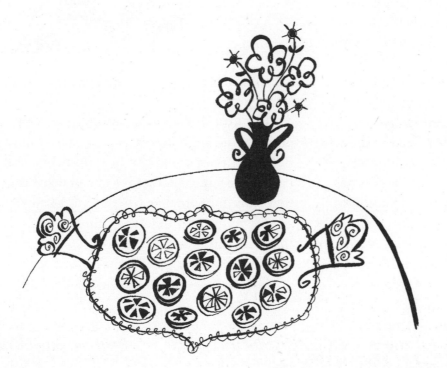

Breads and Breakfast Foods

O F COURSE BREAD AND BREAKFAST don't go together automatically: that's *bed* and breakfast. (Someday I plan to open a "Breakfast and Bed," where guests can go right back to bed after breakfast. There is no more satisfying sleep than a post-breakfast nap.) But I myself can't start the day without eating some kind of flour-based baked good.

My primary requirement for a good breakfast is that it wake people up without scaring them. *Huevos rancheros* would not, for me, meet this requirement. I think that greeting the day with *huevos rancheros* would be like attending a 7:00 A.M. screening of "The Texas Chain-Saw Massacres." Kippers would present a similar problem, although I'd happily eat smoked salmon for breakfast every day if my husband didn't always finish it first. He often has fruit salad for breakfast too. I can't manage that; fruit salad has too much texture for me first thing in the morning. Especially those chopped apples. (As my husband once said, "What's worse in fruit salad than apples?" His friend Maria answered, "Bananas.")

A small amount of breakfast novelty is okay though. Grapefruit gelatin (page 179) is more interesting than plain juice, and recently I've started eating sorbets for the same reason. I love leftover desserts for breakfast. In fact, I always

bake an extra peach pie so we can eat it in the morning.

But I sometimes lose out on things like peach pie and smoked salmon because I tend to sleep later than the rest of my family. I'm still trying to decide whether it's fair to insist that they leave me some, or whether it's so corrupt to sleep late that all I deserve when I wake up is that stale cereal fuzz at the bottom of the Corn Pops box.

For the recipes in this book, I'd wake up on time. Maybe I'd even wake up before everyone else, so that I could get more than they. And then, when I'd eaten up everything good, I'd go back to bed.

Recipes

Mrs. Westerman's Almond Pastry 34

Bagels 36

Onion, Cheddar and Chive Biscuits 39

Herb Biscuits 41

Pumpkin Biscuits 43

Sour Cream Coffee Cake 44

Plain Crackers 46

English Muffin Bread 47

The Greatest Garlic Bread 48

Corn Muffins 49

Seven-Glazed Lemon-Poppy Seed Muffins 51

Oatcakes 53

Popovers 54

Soda Bread 56

The Only Waffles 58

Mrs. Westerman's Almond Pastry

WHERE IS MRS. WESTERMAN THESE DAYS? When I was growing up, she was a friend of my mother's who made wonderful Christmas ornaments and also this wonderful almond pastry. In one cookbook I've seen, this recipe is called "Spanish Breakfast Pastry." I beg to differ! Mrs. Westerman is not Spanish!

Her non-Spanish pastry sounds odd when you read through it. Cream puff pastry baked on top of pie pastry, with frosting on top? *I think not*, you're saying, especially when you see that this recipe is a tiny bit involved to make. But don't listen to yourself. At a recent brunch where we served three kinds of pastry, this was the only one that got eaten all up. It's really delicious.

First Layer

1	cup all-purpose flour
	Pinch of salt
½	cup (1 stick) unsalted butter, chilled and cut into 8 slices
1-2	tablespoons ice water
½	teaspoon vanilla extract

Second Layer

1	cup water
½	cup (1 stick) unsalted butter
1	cup all-purpose flour
3	large eggs, at room temperature (this is important)
1	teaspoon almond extract

Topping

¼	cup (½ stick) unsalted butter, softened
1½	cups confectioners' sugar
2	tablespoons hot milk
1	teaspoon vanilla extract
	Pinch of salt
½	cup sliced almonds, toasted

First layer: In a medium bowl, stir together the flour and salt. With a pastry blender or 2 knives, cut the butter into the flour until it resembles cornmeal. Add the water and vanilla extract and toss the dough with a fork until it forms a ball.

Divide the ball of dough in half. On an ungreased cookie sheet, with your fingertips, pat out each half into a strip about 1 foot long and 3 inches wide. Make sure the strips are a couple of inches apart. Chill the cookie sheet while you get started on the next step.

Second layer: Preheat the oven to 350 degrees F.

Bring the water to a boil in a medium saucepan, add the butter and stir the water briskly until all the butter is melted. Turn down the heat as low as you can. Dump in all the flour at once and stir fast and furiously until the mixture is smooth. Turn off the heat but keep the pan on the burner. Add the eggs, one at a time, beating until the mixture is completely smooth before adding the next egg. Take the pan off the burner and stir in the almond extract.

Divide the egg mixture—which is technically known as *pâte à choux*—into halves. Spread each half over the unbaked pastry strips. If the *choux* gunk is too stiff to spread easily, try wetting your (clean) hands and patting it into shape with your fingers. Make sure that you spread the *choux* right to the edges of each pastry strip.

Bake the 2 strips for 50 to 60 minutes, until they are puffed and just barely brown. The top part will fall slightly as it starts to cool, which is okay. Let the pastry cool while you make the topping.

Topping: In yet another medium saucepan, over low heat, cook the butter until it begins to turn a light caramel color, about 5 minutes. Stir in the confectioners' sugar, milk, vanilla extract and salt and beat until smooth. Divide the topping in half, spread each half over the 2 pastries and sprinkle each pastry with half of the toasted almonds.

To serve, cut the pastries into 1-inch slices. The slices will look prettier if you cut them on the diagonal, but that's not essential.

Serves 10 to 12 brunchers.

"I think not, you're saying. Don't listen to yourself."

Bagels

THIS RECIPE IS ONLY FOR OBSESSIVE COOKS or people who can't get decent bagels where they live. Alas, most of us meet the latter qualification, but how many of us want to make perfect bagels so badly that we're willing to seek out non-diastatic malt powder to put into them? (That's the sweetener the pros use in bagels—not the malted milk kind.) For those who *do*—and if you do, I promise this recipe will not disappoint you—the King Arthur Flour catalog can sell it to you quite easily. If you're not on their mailing list, get on it right away. (See Leftovers, page 199.) In addition to malt powder, bread flour and parchment paper—also called baking parchment—are essential in this recipe. Don't *think* of starting without them.

I haven't scared you off, have I? Because these really are wonderful—chewy, crusty and not puffy and horrible like the bagels you can buy in the freezer section. It was kind of dumb of me to perfect the recipe back when I lived in New York City, but now I *need* it. Although I've adapted this recipe from several sources, I'm indebted to Helen Witty and Elizabeth Schneider for the method, which appeared in their book *Better than Store-Bought*.

Bagel Dough
- 2 cups lukewarm water
- 1 teaspoon sugar
- 1 package active dry yeast
- 5 cups high-gluten bread flour
- ¼ cup non-diastatic malt powder
- 1 tablespoon sugar
- 2 teaspoons salt

Water Bath
- 3 quarts water
- 3 tablespoons sugar
- 3 tablespoons non-diastatic malt powder
- 1 teaspoon salt

Bagel dough: In a small bowl, stir together ½ cup of the water, the sugar and the yeast. Let stand in a warm spot for 10 minutes, or until the yeast has foamed.

In the large bowl of an electric mixer, put 2½ cups of the flour, the malt powder, the sugar, the salt and the remaining 1½ cups water. Combine the ingredients well. Add the yeast mixture and beat everything for 5 minutes. (Alternatively, put the ingredients in a large bowl and beat vigorously by hand.) You now have what in breadmaking circles is known as a sponge.

In a warm place, let the sponge rise for at least 3 hours, or until it collapses back to its former level. (You'll be able to tell when it has done this because you'll see about an inch-thick rim of "collapsed dough leavings" lining the bowl above the dough.) Depending on *how* warm your warm place is, this process may take up to 8 hours. It will happen eventually, so don't worry.

Now add the remaining 2½ cups flour to the collapsed sponge. Knead the dough one way or another: either use the kneading attachment of your mixer, process the dough in your food processor or do it by hand if you must. I do it in a food processor, and it takes 3 minutes of kneading *after* the dough has formed a ball. In any case, the final product should be utterly smooth and faintly shiny.

Put this beautiful dough in an ungreased bowl. Cover with a damp cloth and let it rise in a warm place until it's doubled in bulk. This generally takes only 1 to 2 hours.

Punch down the dough, or let your children do it if you're feeling nice. Shape the dough into a log, place it on a sheet of parchment paper and cut it into 12 equal pieces. Cover the pieces with plastic wrap and let them rest for 15 minutes.

Now take out 1 piece of dough at a time, leaving the rest covered. On a sheet of parchment paper, roll the dough into a 10-inch-long log. Dip each end of the log into warm water and pinch the ends together, working them with your fingers until they're absolutely securely fastened. Now you've achieved a bagel-shaped item. As you work the dough, be sure that the bagel's hole stays at least 1½ inches in diameter; otherwise the bagel will close up when you "bathe" it in the next step. You may need to yank the dough around a bit to maintain the correct hole size. It isn't easy; the dough is quite elastic at this point. But do the best you can.

(continued)

Put each pre-bagel onto yet another sheet of parchment.

Water bath: When all 12 pieces have been shaped, heat the ingredients for the water bath in a large pot. Also, preheat the oven to 400 degrees F, with a rack in the middle.

When the water bath ingredients have reached a low simmer, drop 2 or 3 bagels at a time into the water. Simmer the bagels for 2 minutes on each side, turning them carefully with a slotted spoon. This is what makes that nice, shiny, chewy crust. Don't have a heart attack if a few of the bagels' ends separate, turning your lovely rings into crescents; you'll do better next time, and they'll still taste bagel-y.

Hold a dish towel under the slotted spoon as you remove each bagel. Place the bagels on a large (at least 14-x-17-inch) cookie sheet covered with a *double* sheet of baking parchment.

Bake the bagels in the middle of the oven for 10 minutes. Then turn them over and bake for another 10 minutes or so, until the bagels are well browned. Cool them on a rack. Freeze them if you're not planning to eat them within 24 hours.

Makes 12 bagels.

To turn these into

Cinnamon-Raisin Bagels

Follow the directions above, but add 2 tablespoons of honey to the dough ingredients along with the sugar and malt powder. When you've kneaded the "second dough" (not the sponge) into a smooth, shiny mass, work into it 1 tablespoon of ground cinnamon and ½ cup dark raisins. This will take some doing, as the dough is stiff. But the cinnamon doesn't need to be fully blended into the dough; one of the good things about cinnamon-raisin bagels is those ribbons of cinnamon running through them.

Once you've worked in the raisins and cinnamon, let the dough rise until it's doubled in bulk. Now you're back on track and can continue as above, punching down the dough and dividing it into 12 equal pieces.

> "I haven't scared you off, have I? Because these really are wonderful."

Onion, Cheddar and Chive Biscuits

I REALIZE THAT THIS IS AN IMMENSELY LONG RECIPE just for biscuits. Don't let that stop you. Everyone will love these, and at least the dough can be mixed ahead of time.

Well, everyone who loves strongly flavored, dense, oniony biscuits will love these, anyway. Maybe the biscuits should be renamed. Salad-in-a-Biscuit? I suppose not. Cheese-Vinegar Moisties? No, no. Just be aware that they're quite potent, for a biscuit.

I serve these on summer nights when we're having something grilled.

½	cup (1 stick) unsalted butter, chilled
1	medium red onion, diced (about ½ cup)
½	cup balsamic vinegar
2	cups all-purpose flour
2	tablespoons sugar
1	tablespoon baking powder
1	teaspoon freshly ground pepper
½	teaspoon salt
1	"shake" of cayenne
½	cup snipped fresh chives or scallions (green parts only)
1	cup grated extra-sharp Cheddar
½	cup milk

Preheat the oven to 400 degrees F, with a rack in the middle. Butter a cookie sheet.

In a medium nonreactive skillet, over medium heat, melt 2 tablespoons of the butter. Add the onion and cook it until it's softened and beginning to brown, about 10 minutes. Add the vinegar. Stirring constantly, continue to cook until the vinegar has reduced enough to coat the onions, 5 to 8 minutes. There should be virtually no liquid left in the pan.

Cool the onion-vinegar mixture until it's lukewarm.

In a medium bowl, stir together the flour, sugar, baking powder, pepper, salt and cayenne. With a pastry blender or 2 knives, cut in the remaining 6 tablespoons butter until the mixture looks like coarse cornmeal. Add the cooled onion mixture, chives, cheese and milk. Toss everything together with a fork until the mixture forms a ball. If necessary, add another tablespoon or so of milk.

On a floured surface, knead the dough 12 times. With a floured rolling pin or floured hands, roll or pat out the dough ½ inch thick. (You may need to use a heavy hand with the flour, as this dough is quite moist.) With a floured 2-inch biscuit cutter, cut out biscuits and place them on the cookie sheet. Their sides should not touch. Gather and press together the scraps; reroll them and cut out more biscuits. If you'd like to stop at this point, refrigerate the biscuits until you're ready to bake them.

Bake the biscuits for about 20 minutes (25 to 30 minutes, if they've been refrigerated). Check them after 15 minutes. Since they're already brown from the vinegar, you'll probably have to break one open to see if they're actually done. Once they *are* done, serve them immediately.

Makes 12 to 15 biscuits.

"Be aware that these are quite potent, for biscuits."

Herb Biscuits

S ARAH GAEDE, creator of this recipe, is my new best friend. I haven't met her yet, but she sent me a copy of a cookbook she'd written, and we instantly realized we were long-lost sisters.

As Sarah writes, "I couldn't believe this recipe could be any good, but it is fabulous, especially with fresh herbs." It really is far greater than the sum of its parts. You can use any herb or herbs you want in these biscuits. Thyme is my own favorite, but my daughter Laura has requested that I say that the biscuits are also good without any herbs at all. (But they're really better *with* herbs, Laura.)

You don't necessarily want to tell people how you made these. First, you'd have to confess that they were based on Hungry Jack refrigerated biscuits; second, you'd have to confess that you'd used a rather large amount of butter to make them. Just serve them quietly and listen to everyone go crazy.

> ½   **cup (1 stick) unsalted butter, melted**
> 2   **tablespoons finely chopped fresh herbs of your choice,**
>   **or 1 teaspoon dried**
> 2   **tubes of 10 Hungry Jack Flaky Biscuits**

Preheat the oven to 375 degrees F, with a rack in the middle. Spray the entire inside of a Bundt pan with vegetable-oil spray, or butter it well. Pour the melted butter into the pan and sprinkle it with the herbs. Stand the biscuits on edge all around the pan, as if you were putting plates into a (round) dishwasher.

Bake them in the middle of the oven for 20 to 25 minutes, or until golden brown; allow 5 minutes between removing them from the oven and actually serving them.

When the biscuits are done, turn the Bundt pan over onto an edged cookie sheet or pan; leave it that way for 5 minutes. (Some melted butter will drop out, and you don't want it all over the counter.) Lift the pan off the biscuits and carefully transfer the "cake" of biscuits to a serving platter. Pull the biscuits apart to eat.

Makes 20 very rich biscuits.

(continued)

Variation

This recipe inspired me to create a variation that's also based on refrigerated dough and is also extremely popular with everyone who tries it. (And I'm also extremely mute with guests on how *these* are made.) Substitute two 8-ounce tubes of French bread dough for the biscuits, and use only ½ stick of unsalted butter. Melt the butter in a saucepan. Form the bread dough into golf-ball-sized balls. Roll each ball liberally in the butter, then dip it into freshly grated Parmesan. Place the balls of dough—cheese side up—in a 9-inch square pan, with their sides touching. Bake for 20 to 25 minutes at 375 degrees F, or until golden brown.

Pumpkin Biscuits

THESE ARE AN ADAPTATION of a recipe from Sarah Leah Chase's run-out-and-get-it-right-now-if-you-don't-have-it *Nantucket Open House Cookbook*. My thanks to Ms. Chase for inspiring one Thanksgiving item that my children genuinely like. (As of this writing, John doesn't like turkey, stuffing, mashed potatoes or cranberry sauce; Laura doesn't like stuffing or cranberry sauce and only eats turkey to be polite. Both children shun the relish tray, the gravy and the creamed onions.)

2½	cups all-purpose flour
3	tablespoons packed light brown sugar
1	tablespoon baking powder
½	teaspoon salt
¼	teaspoon *each* freshly ground nutmeg, ground cinnamon and ground ginger
½	cup (1 stick) unsalted butter, chilled and cut into thin slices
1	15-ounce can unsweetened solid-pack pumpkin

Preheat the oven to 400 degrees F, with a rack in the middle. Butter a cookie sheet.

In a large bowl, stir together the dry ingredients. (You may need to crumble the brown sugar with your fingers.) With a pastry blender or 2 knives, cut in the butter until the mixture looks like cornmeal. Stir in the pumpkin and mix until you have a soft dough.

On a well-floured surface, with well-floured hands, pat out the dough until it's ½ inch thick. Using a floured 2-inch biscuit cutter, cut out biscuits. (You can also cut square biscuits with a floured sharp knife.) Place them on the cookie sheet.

Bake the biscuits for 15 to 20 minutes. Because they're already brown, you may need to break one open to see if they're done. Serve hot.

Makes about 36 round biscuits or 16 to 18 square ones.

Sour Cream Coffee Cake

I LOVE SOUR CREAM COFFEE CAKES, but sometimes they're too heavy and doughy; you get the feeling they'd actually be lighter if you just ate the unbaked batter. Reading the recipe for Sarah Gaede's Sour Cream Pound Cake inspired me to try it as the base for a coffee cake, and I was delighted with the results. This coffee cake is moist but fine-textured. The way we serve it at my house is, we put it on the table at breakfast time and leave it there, cutting off hunks of it for the next couple of days until it's gone.

I had to use cardamom once when I realized I was out of cinnamon. We liked it so much that I always add a little cardamom to the cake now.

- 2 cups finely chopped pecans, toasted
- ¾ cup sugar
- 1 tablespoon ground cinnamon
- ½ teaspoon ground cardamom (optional)
- ¼ teaspoon freshly grated nutmeg
- 6 large eggs, at room temperature
- 1 8-ounce container sour cream, at room temperature
- 1 teaspoon vanilla extract
- ½ teaspoon almond extract
- 3 cups sifted all-purpose flour (Sarah specifies White Lily)
- 3 cups superfine sugar (see page 201)
- ½ teaspoon baking soda
- ½ teaspoon salt
- 1 cup (2 sticks) unsalted butter, softened

Preheat the oven to 350 degrees F, with a rack in the middle. Lavishly butter and flour a 10-inch Bundt pan.

In a small bowl, mix together the nuts, sugar, cinnamon, cardamom and nutmeg.

In a medium bowl, whisk together the eggs, sour cream and vanilla and almond extracts. Put the flour, sugar, baking soda and salt in a large bowl. With an electric mixer, beat them at low speed for 30 seconds. Add the butter and half of the egg mixture and mix at low speed until all the dry ingredients are moistened.

Turn the mixer speed to medium and beat for 1 minute. Scrape down the sides. Gradually add the remaining egg mixture in 2 batches, beating for 20 seconds after each addition. Scrape down the sides and beat for 20 more seconds.

Scatter one-quarter of the nut mixture around the bottom of the Bundt pan; pour/scrape one-third of the batter into the pan. Sprinkle the second quarter of the nut mixture onto the batter. Top this with the second third of the batter, top *that* with the third quarter of the nut mixture, top *that* with the last third of the *batter*, and scatter the remaining nut mixture on top of the batter.

Bake the cake for 1 hour, or until a toothpick inserted into the center comes out clean. If the cake doesn't seem done, leave the oven door open for 30 seconds as you turn down the heat to 300 degrees F. Close the door and bake the cake for up to 15 more minutes. Mine takes exactly 1 hour at 350 degrees and 10 minutes at 300 degrees, but my Bundt pan is very lightweight. Cool the cake in the pan on a wire rack for 20 minutes. Turn it out onto the rack, cool it for 10 more minutes and serve.

Makes 1 large coffee cake, serving 12.

Plain Crackers

WHY MAKE YOUR OWN? It's not something you'd want to do all the time, obviously. But for maximum guest intimidation, there's absolutely nothing like homemade crackers. They're no harder to make than cookies, and you can just casually bring them out as though you do this kind of thing all the time. (I have a recipe for homemade soap, too, but I haven't gotten around to making it yet.)

This recipe is very simple. If you were buying the crackers from a country store, they'd be called "common" crackers.

4	cups all-purpose flour
2	tablespoons sugar
1	teaspoon salt
¼	cup (½ stick) unsalted butter
1	cup milk, plus extra for brushing the cracker tops
	Salt (optional)

Preheat the oven to 425 degrees F, with a rack in the middle.

Into a large bowl, sift together the flour, sugar and salt. Cut in the butter with a pastry blender or 2 knives until it looks like cornmeal. Stir in the milk until the homemade dough forms a ball. The dough will be quite stiff.

On a lightly floured board, with a lightly floured rolling pin, roll out the dough ⅛ inch thick. With a 2-inch round cookie cutter dipped in flour, cut out round crackers. Place them on an ungreased cookie sheet. Prick the top of each cracker in several places with a fork. (Making the "fork lines" charmingly askew will emphasize that these are handmade.) Brush the top of each cracker with milk and, if you like, sprinkle each with salt.

Bake the crackers for 15 to 20 minutes, or until they're light gold. Cool them on a rack and store them airtight at room temperature.

Makes around 3½ dozen.

"For maximum guest intimidation, there's nothing like homemade crackers."

English Muffin Bread

JUST BECAUSE RECIPES appear in magazine ads doesn't mean they're not good. *This* recipe made the rounds about 15 years ago, but it's worth yanking out of the file again.

Excuse me, that should be, "It's worth reverently lifting out of the file again." The bread's not exactly "*English muffins in a loaf!*" as the recipe proclaims, but it really does have nice little tunnels inside, like English muffins. And it's easier than making good English muffins from scratch, a task I haven't yet mastered. Anyone out there have a good recipe? Please?

	Cornmeal for sprinkling the pan
5½-6	**cups bread flour**
2	**envelopes active dry yeast**
1	**tablespoon sugar**
2	**teaspoons salt**
¼	**teaspoon baking soda**
2	**cups milk**
½	**cup water**

Butter two 8½-x-4½-inch loaf pans and sprinkle them lavishly with cornmeal.

In a large bowl, combine 3 cups of the flour, the yeast, sugar, salt and the baking soda. In a medium saucepan, heat the milk and water until warm to the touch (120 degrees F); add them to the dry mixture and beat well. Stir in enough of the remaining flour to make a stiff batter.

Spoon the batter into the pans, dividing equally, and sprinkle the batter with more cornmeal. Cover the pans with a damp cloth or plastic wrap. Let the loaves rise in a warm place for 45 minutes. About 20 minutes before they're finished rising, preheat the oven to 400 degrees F, with a rack in the middle.

Bake the loaves for 25 minutes, or until well browned. Remove them from the pans immediately and cool them on racks. Toast each slice before serving.

Makes 2 loaves, 16 slices each.

The Greatest Garlic Bread

THERE'S NO EXCUSE for garlic bread, I know, but as long as you're going to make it—and you are, and so am I—you might as well have the right recipe. *Don't* leave out the lemon-pepper seasoning; it's exactly what the recipe needs.

½	cup (1 stick) unsalted butter, softened
3	large garlic cloves, minced
2	tablespoons mayonnaise
3	tablespoons grated Parmesan
1	teaspoon minced fresh parsley
1	teaspoon dried basil
¼	teaspoon dried oregano
½	teaspoon lemon-pepper seasoning
1	1-pound loaf Italian bread, cut into 1-inch slices

Preheat the oven to 375 degrees F, with a rack in the middle. Line a cookie sheet with foil.

In a small bowl, with an electric mixer, or in a food processor, combine all the ingredients except the bread. (*Duh!* As if you're going to drop a whole loaf of bread in!) Mix everything well. Spread the slices of bread with the garlic-butter mixture and place them on the cookie sheet.

Bake until the edges are browned, about 10 to 12 minutes. Serve immediately.

Makes 1 loaf.

Corn Muffins

Y<small>OU CAN NOW BUY SPECIAL MUFFIN PANS</small> that will bake a muffin that's about 80 percent "crown," or top, with almost none of that boring muffin bottom. I was about to buy such a pan when I realized that I didn't feel right about it. Would a muffin top really taste as good if you didn't have the rest of the muffin to contrast it with? And what about those of us who like to start at the bottom of the muffin and work our way up so that the top is dessert? We wouldn't have anything to do!

However, one nice thing about these corn muffins is that they rise high enough to give you plenty of crown. Another is their taste; they're definitely sweet, and very corny. The crunchy topping—the crown's crown?—is good too.

1	cup milk
½	cup yellow cornmeal, plus 2 tablespoons, plus 1-2 tablespoons for sprinkling on the muffins
2¼	cups all-purpose flour
2	teaspoons baking powder
1	teaspoon baking soda
¼	teaspoon salt
½	cup (1 stick) unsalted butter, softened, plus 2 tablespoons, melted
¾	cup sugar
2	large eggs, beaten
½	teaspoon vanilla extract

Preheat the oven to 400 degrees F, with a rack in the middle. Line a 12-cup muffin pan with paper liners.

In a small saucepan, over low heat, whisk together the milk and the ½ cup cornmeal until they form a lump-free, lukewarm mixture.

In a small bowl, stir together the 2 tablespoons cornmeal, flour, baking powder, baking soda and salt.

(continued)

In a medium bowl, with an electric mixer on medium speed, cream together the ½ cup butter and sugar until light and fluffy. Beat in the eggs and vanilla extract. Now stop using the mixer and start using a whisk or wooden spoon. Thoroughly whisk the milk mixture into the butter mixture. Whisk in the dry ingredients just until the batter is smooth.

Scoop or spoon the muffin batter into the lined muffin cups, which will be almost completely filled. (I use an actual "muffin scoop;" see Leftovers, page 201, for details.) With a pastry brush, gently "paint" the surface of each muffin with the remaining 2 tablespoons melted butter; sprinkle a pinch of cornmeal on top of each muffin.

Bake the muffins for 15 minutes. Lower the heat to 350 degrees and continue baking the muffins for 5 to 10 more minutes, or until they are golden brown. A toothpick inserted into the center of a muffin should come out clean.

Turn out the muffins onto a rack to cool slightly and serve them warm.

Makes 12 muffins.

"Would a muffin top really taste as good if you didn't have the rest of the muffin to contrast it with?"

Seven-Glazed Lemon-Poppy Seed Muffins

L EMON-POPPY SEED MUFFINS are such a staple in bakeries that you'd think there would be lots of recipes for them. But no—I couldn't find a single one in any of my cookbooks, even the regional ones. So, *as usual*, I had to do everything myself. As I once said to my mother when I was three and she had asked me to hang up a towel, "Work, work, work! When will I ever get my rest?"

At first I thought I'd made too much glaze for these, but once I'd glazed each muffin six times, I'd used it all up. (One day I hope to perfect a muffin that consists of nothing *but* glaze.) The "seventh" glaze is the big pinch of sugar you put on top before baking the muffins. If you feel this doesn't count, then go ahead and call them "six-glazed." You will need paper cupcake liners for this recipe; it won't work without them, believe me.

Muffins

2	cups all-purpose flour
2	teaspoons baking powder
	Pinch of salt
6	tablespoons unsalted butter, softened
1	cup sugar, plus more for sprinkling on top of the muffins
2	large eggs, lightly beaten
	Grated rind of 1 large lemon
3	tablespoons poppy seeds
½	cup sour cream
¼	cup fresh lemon juice

Glaze

⅓	cup fresh lemon juice
⅓	cup sugar (superfine works best but isn't essential; see page 201)

Muffins: Preheat the oven to 400 degrees F, with a rack in the middle. Line a 12-cup muffin pan with paper liners.

(continued)

In a small bowl, stir together the flour, baking powder and salt until they're well blended. Set aside.

In a medium bowl, with an electric mixer on medium speed, cream together the butter and 1 cup of the sugar until fluffy. Add the eggs, lemon rind and poppy seeds; beat well. On low speed, beat in the sour cream, the flour mixture and, last of all, the lemon juice. Don't feel you need to beat the batter forever, but don't underbeat it either. (The old rule that says that you should mix muffin batter only until it's moistened is just plain wrong.)

Fill the muffin cups three-fourths full. Sprinkle each muffin generously with big pinches of sugar.

Bake the muffins for 20 to 25 minutes, checking them a couple of times after 15 minutes have passed. You want them golden, not brown.

Glaze: While the muffins are baking, stir the glaze ingredients together in a small bowl until the sugar dissolves. When the muffins are baked, let them cool in the tin for 3 minutes—but leave the oven on. Then, with a toothpick, poke each muffin in 8 places, making sure you poke right down to the bottom. (You're going to leave the muffins in the tin until they're glazed.)

With a pastry brush, lavishly brush the lemon glaze over each muffin. Repeat this process 5 more times. When you're done glazing the muffins, stick the tin back into the oven for 1 more minute to set the glaze a bit. Then cool the muffins, remove them gingerly from the now-quite-sticky muffin tin and serve them.

Makes 12 "muffin-sized" muffins.

"Work, work, work! When will I ever get my rest?"

Oatcakes . . .

WHICH I THINK IS A BETTER NAME than Oatmeal Pancakes. Oatmeal pancakes is what these really are, though—or would "oatjacks" be better? Anyway, they're delicious. Usually I decide to make pancakes about an hour after everyone's woken up on a Saturday morning, which means that we're not finished eating until about an hour after *that*. But you start the batter for these the night before, which helps you jump-start breakfast the next morning. They are dense and moist, reminiscent of the oatmeal from which they sprang. I don't like maple syrup on pancakes, so I sweeten the batter a little—not enough to spoil syrup for anyone else though.

2 **cups old-fashioned rolled oats**
2 **cups milk**
2 **tablespoons packed light brown sugar**
½ **teaspoon salt**
¼ **teaspoon ground cinnamon**
 A few gratings of nutmeg
3 **large eggs**
½ **teaspoon vanilla extract**
6 **tablespoons (¾ stick) unsalted butter, plus more for frying the pancakes**
½ **cup all-purpose flour**
1½ **teaspoons baking powder**

The night before: In a large bowl, stir together the oats, milk, brown sugar, salt and spices. Cover the mixture and refrigerate it overnight.

The next morning: Beat the eggs well and add the vanilla extract. Melt the butter. Sift the flour and baking powder together. Add to the oatmeal mixture along with the melted butter and the beaten eggs. Mix well. Cook like regular pancakes on a hot, greased griddle—not *too* hot, though, or they'll get over-brown before they're cooked through. (You can add more milk if you like thinner pancakes.) Serve with butter and syrup. Blueberry syrup's very good with these; chopped apple is very good *in* these, and so are chopped peaches. I'm sure you can think of other variations.

Makes 16 four-inch pancakes.

Popovers

D ON'T FRET TOO MUCH ABOUT NOODLES," Peg Bracken advised in *The I Hate to Cook Book*. "Whatever you do to them, they remain noodle-like, which Providence probably intended."

The same is true of popovers. Popovers are meant to be a conservative Yankee food. You can't jazz them up too much, or they'll lose their essential comforting quality. I've seen popover recipes that call for chives, and ones that call for chunks of goat cheese, and none of them seems quite popoverish enough. There's some proverb about not putting earrings on an elephant that isn't exactly what I mean, but it comes close enough.

However, using a little whole-wheat flour and a pinch of nutmeg will give your popovers an indefinable ooomph without confusing people. You can't use a lot of whole-wheat flour, or the popovers won't pop.

Some people say the very best popovers are supposed to be started in a cold oven. But that technique has never, never worked for me. Either the popovers stick, or they're as sodden and thick inside as dead frogs. Anyone out there have any suggestions? Until I find out what I'm doing wrong, I'm sticking with a preheated oven.

2-3	tablespoons unsalted butter
1	cup milk
2	large eggs, at room temperature
1	cup all-purpose flour, minus 1 tablespoon
1	tablespoon whole-wheat flour
¼	teaspoon salt
⅛	teaspoon freshly grated nutmeg

Preheat the oven to 400 degrees F, with a rack in the middle. Lavishly grease six 6-ounce custard cups with 1 to 2 tablespoons of the butter; there's nothing more maddening than popovers that "pop" but then refuse to unmold.

Melt the remaining 1 tablespoon of butter. In a small bowl, combine the melted butter with the milk.

Put the eggs, flours, salt and nutmeg into a medium bowl—or a large measuring cup with a pouring spout, which will make it easier to pour the batter neatly. Whisk the milk and butter into the flour mixture until you've achieved a batter, but don't bother getting rid of every single lump. Pour the popover batter into the custard cups, filling each cup halfway.

Bake the popovers for 35 to 40 minutes. Unless you have a glass oven door, DON'T PEEK AT THE POPOVERS until 35 minutes have passed, or they might collapse.

When the popovers are well browned and rigid to the touch, slip them out of the custard cups. Make sure both of your hands are well blanketed in potholders—those custard cups look so grabbable, but they're so hot!

Serve the popovers immediately.

Makes 6 popovers.

Soda Bread

Tisha Hamilton, who gave me this recipe, is a devoted foodie, and we've faxed recipes back and forth over the years. "Judging by the voraciousness with which people devour this whenever I make it, everyone should have a good Irish soda bread recipe," she wrote me, or rather faxed me, recently. "My French au pair, Corinne, finds this especially irresistible—and you know the French are major breadheads." She adds, "If you really like seeds/raisins, you can double either or both with impunity.

"I've always divided this into loaf pans," says Tisha. "But recently I dumped the whole batch into an angel food cake pan, and the result was terrific."

To me, unformedness is part of soda bread's appeal. I don't like to imagine those old Irish cottages with lots of pans all over the place. So I shape the dough into two mounds, as round as I can make them, and bake the mounds on a parchment-lined cookie sheet.

3	cups multigrain flour (available in health-food stores)
1	cup whole-wheat flour
2	tablespoons sugar ("white or brown," Tisha says)
3	teaspoons baking powder
1½	teaspoons baking soda
¼	teaspoon salt
6	tablespoons unsalted butter, chilled and cut into small pieces
1¾	cups buttermilk, plus extra if necessary
1	large egg, beaten
3	tablespoons caraway seeds
¼	cup raisins

Preheat the oven to 350 degrees F, with a rack in the middle. Butter 2 loaf pans, each 5x3x2, or an angel food cake pan, or line a baking sheet with parchment paper.

In a large bowl, stir together the dry ingredients. With a pastry blender or 2 knives, cut in the butter until the mixture resembles coarse crumbs. (You can do both of these steps in a food processor if you'd prefer; if so, dump the mixture into a large bowl as soon as you've processed in the butter.)

Add the buttermilk and egg, mixing in the seeds and raisins as you stir. Add a few more tablespoons of buttermilk if you need them to achieve a soft dough, which is what you want.

Bake the soda bread for 35 to 45 minutes if using loaf pans, for 55 minutes if using an angel food cake pan, or for about 40 minutes if baking free-form. The bread should be brown and crusty all over.

Cool the loaves on a rack. If you're not going to eat the bread within a day or so, you should freeze it. Did you know, by the way, that you should never refrigerate any kind of bread? Refrigerators are too dry for bread. Either freeze it or store it tightly wrapped at room temperature.

Makes 2 loaves, each weighing about 1 pound, or 1 large loaf.

"To me, unformedness is part of soda bread's appeal."

The Only Waffles Better Than That Damn Mix

O H, THE STRUGGLE I HAD with these. First, I stepped on our old waffle iron and snapped off the handle. (Our kitchen was being painted and everything in it was piled up on the dining-room floor.) I was happy to buy another waffle iron—the old one had been coated with black, sticky grease—but *then* I had to have a *recipe*, didn't I? I tried buttermilk waffles, but they were flabby. I tried yeast waffles. "What do you think?" I asked my husband. "Gummy. Tastes like a piece of toast," he said unpromisingly.

My main trouble was coming up with something that actually improved on Pepperidge Farm's Homestyle Pancake and Waffle Mix. I mean, geez—Pepperidge Farm uses, like, 60 kinds of flour! Every time I'd give my family a blind taste test of my own recipe and the mix, they'd pick the mix. Finally, *finally*, I came up with one that they said was equal to the mix. And when my friend Amy said she preferred my recipe, I decided to quit while I was ahead. After all, I had already racked up quite a list of ingredients myself.

Let me just say here that in a blind taste test judged by my family, *I* preferred my own recipe. I did.

2	teaspoons sugar
1	teaspoon active dry yeast
½	cup lukewarm water
2	cups lukewarm milk
½	cup (1 stick) unsalted butter, melted (see note)
2	large eggs, beaten well
2	tablespoons pure maple syrup
1	teaspoon salt
	A few gratings of nutmeg
½	teaspoon vanilla extract
2	cups all-purpose flour
¼	cup *each* whole-wheat flour and rye flour (you can just use ½ cup whole-wheat flour, but the rye really adds something)

2   tablespoons cornmeal
Pinch of baking soda

In a large mixing bowl, stir together the sugar, yeast and water. Let the mixture stand for 5 minutes, or until the yeast has foamed.

Beat in the milk, melted butter, eggs, maple syrup, salt, nutmeg and vanilla extract. In a small bowl, stir together the flours, cornmeal and baking soda. Whisk the dry ingredients into the wet ones, mixing well.

Cook the waffles according to the directions on your waffle iron. They will not be crisp all the way through, because I don't like that kind of waffle. Serve immediately.

Makes about 8 waffles—but waffle irons vary so much in size that I can't be more specific. However, this quantity should at least provide "firsts" for 4 people.

Note: My husband uses 6 tablespoons of melted butter and 2 tablespoons of walnut oil in this recipe. I snarled with disgust when he told me this, but the result is actually really, really great. Sorry I was so mean, Dave.

"I mean, geez—
Pepperidge
Farm uses,
like, 60 kinds
of flour!"

Soups and Sandwiches

Shouldn't that be "Soups 'n' Sandwiches"? Or "Soups, Sips, Salads and Sides," like the chapter in the cookbook put out by the board of my daughter's nursery school? But anyway, soups and sandwiches. This is kind of a small section. I don't make many soups because for many years the only soup my kids would eat was canned chicken noodle poured into a sieve and rinsed with cold water until all the broth was gone. "What's *this*?" my daughter once asked in amazement when someone served her a conventional bowl of chicken noodle soup. That was a long time ago, but we haven't quite morphed into one of those families that has soup for supper. When we do, I'm counting on people to give me good recipes.

You don't really need recipes for sandwiches, do you? Good, because there is only one in this section. Maybe I'm alone in this, but I feel as though a sandwich isn't something you *plan*. You don't go out and buy ingredients for it; you make it with whatever you have in the house. Meat loaf, apricot preserves, creamed onions, whatever. For many people, Thanksgiving dinner is primarily a route to a week's worth of great sandwiches. For some, a sandwich is just an excuse to eat mayonnaise.

Once, what I had in the house was some bacon and some radicchio, so I made a BLT with bacon, radicchio and little flecks of sun-dried tomatoes. It was delicious, but I wouldn't presume to tell you to make it unless I knew for sure that you had half a head of radicchio in your house.

However, if you feel that you need more sandwich direction, just write and tell me what's in your house, and I'll tell you how to put it between some bread.

60

Recipes

The Best Egg Salad 62

Roast Garlic Corn Chowder 63

Iced Peach Soup 64

Salsa Soup 65

Bacony Split Pea Soup 67

Tomato Soup with Millet 68

The Best Egg Salad
(In Memory of Patty Marx)

PATTY ISN'T AT ALL DEAD. I just named this recipe after her because she kept saying, "You *are* going to put egg salad in the book, aren't you?" Then she kept reminding me to put in bacon—as though *that* was something I needed telling. It's more politically correct to serve this on rye bread or pumpernickel, but if I'm eating it where no one can see me, I just use white.

¾ cup mayonnaise
¼ cup sour cream
3 tablespoons Dijon mustard
¼ teaspoon sweet or hot Hungarian paprika
12 large hard-boiled eggs, peeled and chopped
8 ounces thick-cut bacon, cooked crisp and crumbled
6 scallions, minced
2 tablespoons prepared white horseradish, or to taste
   Salt and freshly ground pepper to taste

In a small bowl, whisk together the mayonnaise, sour cream, mustard and paprika. In a medium bowl, combine the eggs, bacon and scallions, and stir in as much of the mayonnaise dressing as you like. (I use it all.) Add horseradish and salt and pepper to taste.

Makes enough filling for 8 sandwiches. I know there are some people who eat egg salad with a fork, but I'm not one of them. I hope Patty isn't either.

Roast Garlic Corn Chowder

I'M VERY FOND of traditional corn chowder, but I didn't really see the point of trying to track down the best recipe for it. They're all sort of sweet and milky, aren't they? Any recipe for traditional corn chowder will be good as long as you use very fresh corn.

There are a couple of recipes where you add bacon, but even I have to draw the line somewhere; not *all* the recipes in this book can contain bacon. So here's a recipe that goes off in another direction. It's milkish, but not milkoid.

6	large garlic cloves, chopped
1	cup chopped onion
1	cup red bell pepper, finely chopped
2	tablespoons unsalted butter
4	cups fresh corn kernels (about 5 ears' worth); frozen, defrosted is an okay substitute
3	cups chicken broth
1	small jalapeño or serrano chili, seeded and minced
1	cup heavy cream
1	cup milk
	Salt and freshly ground pepper to taste

"This is milkish, but not milkoid."

Preheat the oven to 375 degrees F. Roast the chopped garlic in the oven on a greased surface, stirring occasionally, until it's soft, about 8 to 10 minutes. (I always do this on a little greased snip of foil, so as not to waste a whole pan.) While the garlic is roasting, sauté the onion and bell pepper in the butter until they're softened. You may as well do this in the pot in which you'll be cooking the soup.

Now put the garlic in with the other vegetables. And *now* add the corn, chicken broth and chili pepper. Bring the mixture to a boil, then reduce the heat to low and simmer it for 10 minutes to blend the flavors. Stir in the cream and milk and simmer gently for 1 to 2 minutes; don't let the mixture boil again.

Season the chowder to taste and serve at once.

Serves 4.

Iced Peach Soup

THIS SOUP, along with Grapefruit Gelatin (page 179) and some kind of pastry, makes a perfect summer breakfast for company. My mother, my sister and I once gave a combined library/lingerie breakfast bridal shower featuring that exact menu. It was kind of a lot of themes for one party, but we managed to pull everything together.

But anyway, everyone was enraptured with the soup, or at least they *said* they were. *I* certainly was. The ingredients alchemized into something more complex and subtle than you'd imagine from just reading the recipe. And the soup's blushing, bridal tint was flattering to *all* complexions.

10	large, ripe peaches, peeled, pitted and cut into chunks
1	cup sugar
¼	teaspoon ground cinnamon
	Juice of 2 lemons
1½	cups sour cream
2	cups water
1⅓	cups white wine

In a blender or food processor, puree the peaches, sugar, cinnamon and lemon juice until completely smooth. Pour into a medium bowl. Whisk in the sour cream thoroughly; whisk in the water and the white wine. Chill the soup, covered, for several hours before serving. A few edible flowers—unsprayed, please—make a nice garnish to float on top of the bowl; a crystal punch bowl makes a nice vessel to float the flowers on top of.

Serves 6.

Salsa Soup

THIS IS NOT ONLY DELICIOUS but a very pretty pale peach color. (I'm sorry to keep going on about soups' colors, but you do notice them when they're unusual.) It's almost as good cold as it is hot too. Just don't give in to your baser instincts to serve it with crumbled tortilla chips on top. A few cilantro leaves, artfully placed, will be much more effective.

1   large yellow onion, chopped
2   large garlic cloves, minced
1   small fresh jalapeño chili, seeded and minced
1½   tablespoons unsalted butter
1   28-ounce can whole tomatoes in juice, coarsely chopped
1   28-ounce can crushed tomatoes in thick puree
1   4-ounce jar "hot" salsa
3   ounces cream cheese, cut into chunks
4   cups chicken broth
1   cup light cream
2   tablespoons fresh lime juice, or to taste
½   teaspoon Tabasco, or to taste
3   tablespoons chopped fresh cilantro, or to taste,
     plus whole cilantro leaves for garnish
     Salt and freshly ground pepper to taste

In a large nonreactive pot or Dutch oven, over medium heat, sauté the onion, garlic and jalapeño in the butter until the onion is translucent, about 5 minutes. Add the tomatoes and salsa and cook, stirring frequently, until the liquid has mostly evaporated, about 20 minutes. The mixture will be thick and porridgey, with noisily popping bubbles that spatter the stovetop.

With the heat turned to low, add the cream cheese, chunk by chunk, stirring constantly until it's all melted and mixed in. Stir in the chicken broth, cream, lime juice, Tabasco and cilantro, and heat everything gently. Taste the soup for seasoning; add more lime juice, Tabasco and cilantro, if you want, as well as adding salt and pepper, if you think they're called for.

Serve the soup either hot or cold, floating some cilantro leaves on top of each bowl. You won't get me to say "atop" each bowl, no matter how hard you try.

Serves 6.

"Don't give in to your baser instincts to serve this with crumbled tortilla chips on top."

Bacony Split Pea Soup

I KNOW WE ALL NEED to eat lower on the food chain, and at my house we're trying. Still, there's no denying the fact that any split pea soup tastes a thousand percent better with a hefty dose of smoked meats. This recipe gives you double value—bacon *and* a ham hock.

¼	pound bacon slices
1	large onion, diced
2	large carrots, chopped
1	large garlic clove, minced
1	pound dried split peas, picked over
2½	quarts water
1	smoked ham hock
2	teaspoons freshly ground pepper, or to taste
1	bay leaf
⅛	teaspoon ground allspice

In a heavy kettle or soup pot, over medium heat, cook the bacon until it's crisp. Take the bacon out of the pot and drain it on paper towels; you won't be using it again until the soup's done. Pour off all but 4 tablespoons of the bacon fat. ("*All but 4 tablespoons?*" I can hear some of you asking in wonderment.)

Over low heat, stirring frequently, cook the onion and carrots in the bacon fat until softened, about 5 minutes. Stir in the rest of the ingredients. Simmer the soup over low heat, uncovered, for 2 hours. You may need to add another cup or so of water if the soup starts to get too thick before the time is up.

Carefully lift the ham hock out of the soup and remove from it what usable meat you can. Chop the meat and return it to the soup pot. Fish out the bay leaf if you can find it. Check the seasoning; it's unlikely you'll need salt, but you might want to add some more pepper or allspice.

Serve each bowl of soup piping hot—I've been waiting to say "piping hot"!—with a few crumbled bits of bacon on top.

Makes 8 cups, serving 4.

Tomato Soup with Millet

MILLET IS ONE OF MY BIRDS' FAVORITE FOODS. However, the millet *you* want is the kind you buy at health-food stores, not bird stores.

Having now caused you to turn the page, let me call you back by saying that this is a great soup, much more interesting and full of stuff than most tomato soups. I'm indebted to Henry Pennell for giving me the original recipe, which he had eaten at the Fiddlehead Restaurant in Juneau, Alaska. I poutingly told him that I already *had* a good tomato-soup recipe in my first cookbook, but luckily he persisted. This recipe is adapted from the one in *The Fiddlehead Cookbook*, which Henry gave me as a present even though I'd been such a pig.

1	tablespoon corn oil
1	cup diced onion
1	cup diced carrots
1	cup diced green bell pepper
½	cup diced celery
1	tablespoon minced garlic
1	28-ounce can tomato puree
1	28-ounce can whole tomatoes in puree
½	cup dry white wine
2	teaspoons minced fresh thyme or ½ teaspoon dried
1	teaspoon freshly ground pepper
1	bay leaf
½	cup chicken broth
2	tablespoons millet
⅓	cup minced fresh flat-leaf parsley
	Salt to taste

Heat the oil in a large nonreactive soup pot over medium heat. Add the onion, carrot, green pepper, celery and garlic. Cook the vegetables, stirring frequently, for 5 to 7 minutes, until the onion is wilted.

Add the tomato puree and the whole tomatoes. Take a big pair of kitchen scissors and coarsely chop the whole tomatoes right in the pot—an easy way to do a messy task. Add the white wine, thyme, pepper and bay leaf.

Bring the soup to a boil, then reduce the heat to low, cover the pot, and simmer the soup for 30 minutes. Stir it once in awhile so it won't stick to the bottom.

As soon as you've covered the soup, put the chicken broth and millet into a small saucepan—preferably a *very* small one. Bring to a boil, cover the saucepan, reduce the heat and cook the millet very, very slowly until the broth is all absorbed and the millet is soft, about 45 minutes. If you need to, add a little water. If, at the end of 30 minutes, all the broth hasn't been absorbed into the millet, uncover the pot until it *has* all been absorbed.

Combine the cooked millet with the cooked soup, making sure to break up any millet-clumps. Stir in the parsley, season with salt and serve the soup right away. If you wait too long, the millet will turn the mixture a bit too thick, which is nice and hearty but perhaps not quite what you want. Tomato soup is one thing; tomato gruel is another.

Makes 1½ quarts, serving 4.

Main Dishes

"I REALLY LIKED MY HAMBURGER," my nephew Charlie once announced, "except for the gray part." The gray part was the hamburger. There must be a family tendency to prefer the gilding to the, uh, picture frame: Charlie's cousin, my daughter, used to call cake the "breading."

Still, over the years, I've tended to agree with Charlie. It can be a challenge to make a big slab of protein interesting. There it sits on your plate, a sullen baked lump, surrounded by all the *fun* parts of the meal: the gemlike appetizers, the half-portions of pasta, the mesclun with its baby leaves, the wine, the desserts . . . . Why not just skip the gray part entirely?

Actually, I often do. These days I find myself making more and more meals that consist only of side dishes. But every once in awhile, I want something that puts its foot down and states, "I am the main course. So there." You know what I mean: something that thuds when you put it on the table.

If it's going to be that bossy, a main dish has to earn its room on the plate. It has to taste good enough to make you forget that it's not composed primarily of grains and legumes. It has to reassure you that square-mealishness does have its place in the psychic realm, and that once in awhile it's nice to leave the table feeling *full*.

These recipes will do that for you.

Recipes

Beef Stew 72

Sticky Chicky 74

Parsley-Parmesan Chicken Breasts 76

Wedding Chicken 78

Mustard-Glazed Flank Steak 79

Two Things You Must Serve with Ham 80

Marinated Butterflied Leg of Lamb 82

Lisa Lasagna's Lasagna 84

Mature Macaroni and Cheese 87

Cold "Barbecued" Pork Loin 89

Pot Roast with Leeks and Brandy 91

The Roast Beef 92

Perfect Salmon 94

Shrimp with Feta and Fennel 96

Cheese Soufflé 98

Tortellini with Pistachio Sauce 100

Perfected Turkey 101

Beef Stew

AN ALMOST IDENTICAL VERSION of this recipe appeared in *Beat This!* Back then, you could still find Campbell's Tomato Bisque Soup. Now you can't, or at least I can't. This has worried a few people who were too timid to substitute Campbell's regular tomato soup on their own. I might have let them figure it out themselves, but I figured that this book could use another main dish. So now it's official: Go ahead and use regular tomato soup.

Don't shy away from this recipe if you're a purist. It's much better than any conventional stovetop stew, even though it does have canned soup in it. Hoping to make it more respectable, I tried substituting canned tomatoes. Nope—it wasn't as good that way. The tomato soup makes a nice meaty gravy.

2	pounds suitable-for-stew beef, cut into cubes
6	carrots, cut into thick slices
2	large onions, chopped coarsely
1	large baking potato, cut into big "stew-size" dice
1	bay leaf
1	teaspoon dried oregano
1	teaspoon salt
½	teaspoon freshly ground pepper
1	10-ounce can Campbell's Tomato Soup
½	soup can water, red wine or beer

Preheat the oven to 275 degrees F.

In a large bowl, combine the beef, carrots, onions, potato and bay leaf. Sprinkle the seasonings over all and mix well. In a small bowl, combine the soup with whatever liquid you choose. Then, wincing, pour the diluted soup over the stew ingredients.

Put everything into a lidded casserole. Cover the casserole first with a tight layer of foil and then with the lid.

Bake the stew for 5 hours. After the first 2 hours, check it every 30 minutes or so to make sure there's enough liquid. There probably will be, but it's no fun to take the lid off when the 5 hours are up and be presented with a scorched pile of glop. Fish out the bay leaf before serving.

Thick-sliced mushrooms would be good in this, as would a handful of chopped parsley added at the end. But don't go crazy. As I said in the Tomato Bisque version, "This is stew you're making, not beef bourguignon."

Serves 6.

"So now it's official: go ahead and use regular tomato soup."

Sticky Chicky

I'M GETTING BOLDER about giving people embarrassing recipes, especially if I'm sure that children will like them. As many of us know, it's not easy to find a recipe that kids love and grownups like—and, as my sister-in-law Anne said when she was little, "This is also vice versa." Sticky Chicky crosses the generations. You wouldn't serve it to company, but your children will love it, and you will find it perfectly acceptable, sort of like sweet-and-sour chicken without those embarrassing pineapple chunks. Also, it's easy and low in fat. Don't I sound like a women's magazine?

The chicken needs to marinate for 24 hours or longer before it's cooked. Rice is mandatory with Sticky Chicky.

> ½ **cup vinegar (I use balsamic, but cider or distilled work too)**
> ½ **cup soy sauce**
> ½ **cup sugar**
> 2 **garlic cloves, crushed**
> 1 **tablespoon grated fresh ginger**
> 3-4 **pounds chicken pieces, preferably with the skin removed, quartered (chicken breasts are my favorite here)**

Combine the vinegar, soy sauce, sugar, garlic and ginger in a shallow baking dish big enough to hold the chicken in a single layer. Stir the marinade until the sugar dissolves. Put the chicken into the dish and turn each piece over a few times to coat well. Cover the baking dish and chill the chicken for 24 hours.

The next day, bring the chicken to room temperature. Transfer the chicken and the marinade to a large heavy skillet. Over medium heat, bring the marinade to a boil. Reduce the heat to low, cover the skillet and simmer the chicken for 15 minutes, turning each piece occasionally. Preheat the oven to 200 degrees F.

Check the chicken breasts for doneness; they will cook faster than the dark pieces and may even be done by now. Keep checking them as you uncover the skillet and cook the chicken for 15 minutes longer, or until the meat is tender and the juices run clear when you prick a piece with a fork. Put the chicken pieces on a platter, cover it with foil and keep it warm in the oven for the final step.

Turn up the heat to medium. Cook the sauce in the skillet until it's syrupy and caramelized, stirring frequently. This will take about 10 to 15 minutes; after 10 minutes, turn the heat back down to low to prevent the sauce from suddenly overcooking. Return the chicken to the skillet, coat it with the sauce, and serve immediately.

Serves 4.

The Best Use of Boned Chicken Breasts: Parsley-Parmesan Chicken Breasts

BONED CHICKEN BREASTS are so easy to use that we tend to forget they're not as good as *unboned* chicken. You can't cook them for a long time, so they won't acquire the character that long braising or baking would give them. You can't cook them in lots of liquid, or their texture gets all rubbery and weird. They don't have as much flavor as bone-in pieces of chicken. Wait a minute—why are we using them?

Well, they're good in chicken salad. And, as I've just said, they're easy. Sometimes you just *have* to make something easy and boneless. It might as well be delicious too.

Another good (and even longer) name for this dish would be Best Chicken Alternate for a Picnic—After Fried Chicken, I Mean.

½   cup Dijon mustard
¼   cup dry white wine or dry vermouth
1   garlic clove, crushed
1   cup fresh bread crumbs
1   cup grated Parmesan
3   tablespoons minced shallots
¼   cup minced fresh parsley
1   tablespoon unsalted butter, melted
¼   teaspoon *each* salt and freshly ground pepper
8   chicken breast halves, boned (about 1½ pounds)

Preheat the oven to 375 degrees F. Line a 13-x-9-inch pan with foil.

In a shallow pan—say, a pie pan—whisk together the mustard, wine or vermouth and garlic. In another shallow pan, thoroughly combine the crumbs, Parmesan, shallots, 3 tablespoons of the parsley, melted butter, salt and pepper.

One at a time, flop each chicken breast around in the mustard-wine mixture until it's coated; roll it in the crumb mixture until it's liberally coated with *that*.

Bake the chicken breasts in the pan for 25 to 30 minutes, or until they're golden brown and cooked through. (To be on the safe side, you might slice into one of them to check. You can always push the crumb topping over the cut part.) Sprinkle the remaining 1 tablespoon of parsley over the chicken and serve immediately.

Or wait until the chicken is room temperature and *then* serve it.

Or let it come to room temperature and chill it and serve it cold. That's where the picnic part would come in, you see.

Serves 4 (if everyone gets seconds) to 6 (if 2 people get seconds) to 8 (if no one gets seconds).

"Sometimes you just *have* to make something easy and boneless."

77

Wedding Chicken

NO COOKBOOK OF MINE (or of *anyone's*, really) would be complete without a recipe from my friend Rebecca Atwater Briccetti. When I asked her for a main dish, she instantly said, "Wedding Chicken. Do you remember it from my wedding?" "No," I answered, "but I had an awful lot of champagne." Now that I've tried the recipe, I feel it would almost be worth getting married again so that I could serve it at *my* wedding.

½   cup mayonnaise
¼   cup plain yogurt
3   canned, flat anchovy fillets, drained
1   tablespoon drained capers
2   tablespoons fresh lemon juice, or to taste
3   whole chicken breasts, halved, boned and poached
1   6½-ounce can white tuna *in oil*, drained
½   cup plus 2 tablespoons fresh basil, cut into thin strips
        (or "chiffonaded," as Rebecca elegantly puts it)
     Thin-sliced lemons for garnish
     Sliced Niçoise olives for garnish

In the bowl of a food processor, process the tuna, mayonnaise, yogurt, anchovies, capers and lemon juice. Fold in the ½ cup basil and chill the sauce for 3 to 4 hours.

Wrap each poached chicken breast tightly in plastic wrap to make a neat little packet. "You *must* do this," Rebecca says. Chill the breasts for at least 2 hours.

Slice each chicken breast on the diagonal and fan the slices slightly on each plate. Nap them with the sauce. Decorate each sauced piece of chicken with the lemon slices, the remaining 2 tablespoons basil and the sliced olives. At least, Rebecca suggests the olives. I hate olives myself, but I can see that they'd look nice on the plate.

Serves 6.

Mustard-Glazed Flank Steak

I SUPPOSE THAT TECHNICALLY you can't glaze something with an un-shiny thing like mustard, but I like the sound of it anyway. I could eat almost any form of flank steak (except for a *boiled* flank steak that food writer/novelist Laurie Colwin once described), but I love this one for sentimental reasons as well as for its taste. The recipe comes from the Rochester Junior League's second cookbook, *For Goodness Taste*, and I come from Rochester.

Maybe that's not enough of an endorsement? I guess you'll just have to try the recipe.

- ⅓ **cup Dijon mustard**
- 2 **tablespoons soy sauce**
- 1 **tablespoon heavy cream**
- 1 **teaspoon dried thyme**
- 1 **teaspoon grated fresh ginger**
- 1 **teaspoon Asian sesame oil**
- ½ **teaspoon freshly ground pepper**
- 2 **large garlic cloves, minced**
- 1 **1-pound flank steak**

Mix the non-steak ingredients in a small bowl and coat the meat on both sides. (Use up all the stuff in the bowl.) Cover the flank steak with plastic wrap and chill it for 18 to 24 hours or up to 48 hours; a tough cut like this takes a long time to absorb flavors.

Bring the steak back to room temperature (a couple of hours should do it). Broil it inside, in a preheated broiler, or grill it outside over hot coals, for 5 minutes a side. (The meat will be medium-rare; feel free to adjust the cooking time if you prefer it less or more well done.) Let the flank steak stand for 5 minutes before slicing it on an angle against the grain.

Serves 3 to 4.

Two Things You Must Serve with Ham

HAM IS TOO COMPLICATED for me to give you a recipe here. I don't mean it's hard to cook: basically all you have to do to a ham is glaze it and stick it in the oven. But how do I know what kind of ham you're going to buy? Will it be bone-in or bone-out? Will it be one of those prebaked spiral-cut ones? Will it be a country ham that you have to soak for about six years to get the salt out? Will it be fresh? (And I hope that it won't, because fresh ham is just like plain pork—not that there's anything wrong with pork, but it's not ham.) I can't make a diagnosis unless I can *see* your ham. Follow the directions on the wrapper, or ask the person who sold it to you, or look up ham in *The Joy of Cooking*.

However, I *can* help you with two mandatory ham procedures. You have to glaze your ham with Pantry Glaze, and you have to serve it with Pantry Mustard. Michael Ackerman kindly gave me the recipes for both.

Pantry Ham Glaze

ABOUT THIS GLAZE, Michael protested, "The recipe is too simple to give you." But it's not; it's perfect. I would never have been able to figure it out if he hadn't told me what was in it. Things don't always have to be complicated to be just right.

½   cup apricot preserves
½   cup Dijon mustard

In a food processor or blender, puree the apricot preserves. Heat the puree gently in a small saucepan and blend in the mustard until smooth. Spread the glaze all over your ham before baking.

Just don't decide to broil the baked ham for a couple of seconds to brown the glaze, and then leave it under the broiler for a couple of *minutes*. That's what I did once, and we ended up with a ham that was crusted in a solid sheet of black ash. The ham underneath was fine, but no one would have called it "glazed."

When the ham is done baking, turn on the broiler. Then leave the oven door ajar and stand right there, watching, until the glaze is as brown as you like. It probably won't take more than 45 seconds. After all, the glaze will have been baking for awhile already.

Pantry Mustard

YOU CAN SERVE THIS MUSTARD with other foods besides ham, and you should. There was a long time when I loved it so much that I ate it straight. Now I'm used to it, so I just use it in cooking—it makes a great marinade for broiled shrimp—and on sandwiches. Plan to chill this mustard for a day before using it.

- ¼ cup coarse-grained mustard
- ¼ cup Dijon mustard
- ¼ cup dried basil leaves
- ½ cup canola oil

In a food processor, blend the mustards and basil leaves until smooth. With the machine running, slowly add the oil until the mixture is smooth. The mustard keeps indefinitely refrigerated; cover it tightly to prevent it from darkening.

Makes about 1 cup.

"Things don't always have to be complicated to be just right."

Marinated Butterflied Leg of Lamb

IT MUST HAVE BEEN THE GREEKS who discovered the lemon-lamb affinity—and what geniuses they were for doing it. This marinade is also wonderful with grilled lamb chops. I assume it would be great for marinating chicken as well; many lamb preparations work with chicken as long as there's no mint jelly involved. But why would there be? Is there anything more hateful than mint jelly? Let's not even think about it.

You'll see that there's relatively little oil in this recipe. Most marinades are greatly improved by cutting the oil to almost nothing. Oil *adds* almost nothing to a marinade, after all; it just cuts the power of the other ingredients. In the days of stringy, fatless, free-range meats, oil in a marinade may have helped the flavor. Nowadays, however, any cut of meat you can buy in a conventional store has more than enough fat right inside it; you don't need to *soak* it in fat as well. Take most of the oil out of any marinade recipe, and I think you'll like the results a lot better.

1	**6-to-7 pound leg of lamb, boned and butterflied**
¼	**cup corn oil**
¼	**soy sauce**
2	**teaspoons grated lemon rind**
½	**cup fresh lemon juice**
3	**garlic cloves, crushed**
¼	**cup minced fresh parsley**
2	**tablespoons fresh rosemary or 1 teaspoon dried**

Arrange the meat so that it lies before you like a messy open book made out of meat. Score the larger slabs ½ inch deep with a sharp knife so that they'll cook at the same rate as the thinner parts.

Lay the lamb flat in a large nonreactive dish. In a small bowl, whisk together the oil, soy sauce, lemon rind, lemon juice, garlic, parsley and rosemary and pour them over the meat. Turn the lamb over a couple of times to coat it with the marinade. Cover the dish with plastic wrap and chill it for 24 to 48 hours, turning the lamb several times; this gives the marinade time to penetrate the meat.

Bring the lamb to room temperature before cooking. (Except in the dead of summer, this will take at least 2 hours.)

It's helpful at this point, though not essential, to skewer the meat from left to right. One skewer should go through the top third of the "book" and one through the bottom third. This will keep the meat more tidy and compact.

To cook the lamb indoors: Preheat the oven to 375 degrees F, with a rack in the upper third. Transfer the meat, boned side up, to a large shallow roasting pan. Pour the marinade over it. Bake it for 20 to 25 minutes, without turning. For rare lamb—the only acceptable way of serving it, really—a meat thermometer inserted into the thickest lobe will read 120 degrees F.

Remove the lamb from the oven and turn up the heat to broil. To make it look more "grilled," put the lamb as close as possible to the broiler element and broil it for 2 minutes, without turning. Transfer it to a carving board and let it rest, covered with foil, for 10 minutes before you carve it. Slice the meat as you would flank steak, against the grain.

To cook the meat on a grill, which is even better: When your coals are at their hottest, transfer the meat to an oiled, double-sided rack and barbecue it for 45 minutes to 1 hour, turning the rack every 5 minutes and brushing the meat with the marinade. For rare meat, cook until a meat thermometer inserted into the thickest lobe reads 120 degrees F. Put the meat onto a carving board and let it rest, covered with foil, for 10 minutes before carving it as above.

Serves 6 to 8.

"Is there anything more hateful than mint jelly?"

Lisa Lasagna's Lasagna

Tʜɪs ɪs ɴᴀᴍᴇᴅ for one of my best friends, Lisa Lasagna. Lisa lives in Victoria, British Columbia. She visits me every fall so that we can go through our old yearbooks and look at cute guys from our high school.

This lasagna takes ages to make. It's totally worth it—I wouldn't give you the recipe if it weren't—but I suggest breaking up its preparation into two days. On the first day, make the sauces, cook the chicken or shrimp, slice the Gruyère, make and crumble the bacon, grate the Parmesan, set the spinach out to thaw and sauté the mushrooms. Wrap or cover everything except the spinach tightly and chill it until the next day. On the next day, do everything else. On the third day, stay in bed.

Tomato Sauce

½	cup minced onions
2	tablespoons corn oil
4	plum tomatoes, peeled, deglopped and chopped
2	cups canned tomatoes in thick puree (Redpack usually wins in blind taste tests)
2	large garlic cloves, minced
1	long strip of orange rind
	Salt and freshly ground pepper to taste

Béchamel Sauce

2	cups milk
2	cups chicken broth
5	large shallots, minced
6	tablespoons (¾ stick) unsalted butter
½	cup all-purpose flour
½	cup dry white wine or vermouth
	A few gratings of nutmeg
	Salt and freshly ground pepper to taste

1   **teaspoon salt**

1   **teaspoon oil**

10-12   **curly lasagna noodles**

2   **10-ounce packages frozen *whole* spinach, thawed**

6   **slices thick-cut bacon, cooked until crisp and crumbled**

3   **cups cooked chopped shrimp or chicken**

2   **cups sliced mushrooms, sautéed until tender in 2 tablespoons unsalted butter (save the liquid)**

½   **teaspoon dried thyme**

1½   **cups 1-inch pieces thinly sliced Gruyère (8 to 10 ounces)**

1   **cup grated Parmesan**

Tomato sauce: In a large saucepan over medium heat, sauté the onion in the oil for 5 minutes, until wilted. Add the fresh tomatoes to the onion and cook, covered, for 5 minutes. Add the canned tomatoes, garlic and orange rind. Half-cover the pan and simmer the sauce for at least 30 minutes, or until it's nice and thick. Season it to taste with salt and pepper.

Béchamel sauce: In a small saucepan, combine the milk and chicken broth and set over low heat. In a large saucepan, over medium heat, sauté the shallots in the butter until they have softened, about 3 minutes. When the butter is bubbling, dump in all the flour at once. Whisk the mixture constantly with a wooden spoon for 2 minutes; don't let it brown.

Gradually stir the hot milk-broth mixture into the shallot mixture, whisking constantly. Add the wine. Then bring the sauce to a boil and, still whisking constantly, cook it until it's thick enough to coat a spoon. Add the nutmeg, salt and pepper. If you're making the béchamel ahead of time, scrape down the sides with a rubber spatula and pour a couple of tablespoons of milk on top of the sauce to keep a skin from forming.

Everything else and Assembly: Preheat the oven to 400 degrees F, with a rack in the upper third.

Bring a big pot of water to a boil. Add the salt and oil to the water; cook the lasagna according to the package directions, 11 to 13 minutes.

(continued)

Squeeze the spinach in a towel to remove every bit of moisture. Using scissors or a sharp knife, chop the spinach. (Never use frozen chopped spinach; it has too much water.) Give the chopped spinach one more wring-out in the towel.

Toss together the bacon and the shrimp or chicken until they're well combined.

When the lasagna is done, drain it well and run cold water over it. Redrain it. Grease a 13-x-9-inch pan well. Stir the cooked mushrooms and their liquid into the béchamel sauce, which will be quite thick if it's been chilled. Stir in the thyme.

Plomp a dollop of béchamel—say, about ⅓ cup—into the bottom of the pan and spread it around with a rubber spatula. Place the first layer of lasagna on the sauce and cover the lasagna with about 1 cup more béchamel. Scatter half of the spinach over the béchamel; scatter half of the meat-bacon mixture over the spinach; scatter half of the Gruyère over the meat; and spoon about ½ cup more béchamel over the Gruyère.

"On the third day, stay in bed."

Apply the second layer of lasagna and repeat the procedure exactly.

Apply the top layer of lasagna and cover it with whatever béchamel is left. Cover *that* with about 2½ cups of the tomato sauce. Cover *that* with the grated Parmesan.

Bake the lasagna for 30 to 40 minutes, until it's bubbling all over and the Parmesan has browned. Let the dish sit for 5 to 10 minutes before you cut it, or you'll be serving everyone lasagna puddles instead of neat squares.

Serves 8.

Mature Macaroni and Cheese

MACARONI AND CHACARONI," we call it at my house. I can't wait for my kids' palates to grow up so we can *always* serve this kind without having to give the plain kind equal time.

1½	cups chicken broth
½	cup dry white wine
3	cups heavy cream
1½	tablespoons unsalted butter
1	medium onion, diced
2	large scallions, minced
2	large garlic cloves, minced
2	teaspoons salt for boiling the pasta
1	pound rotelle pasta (or another shape, if you prefer)
2	tablespoons Dijon mustard
¼	pound extra-sharp Cheddar, grated
¼	pound Gouda, grated
¼	pound Gruyère, grated
	Salt, freshly ground pepper and cayenne to taste
2	ounces Parmesan, finely grated

Preheat the oven to 500 degrees F. Butter a 13-x-9-inch baking dish.

Bring the chicken broth and wine to a boil in a medium saucepan. Over high heat, reduce the mixture to ¾ cup. Bring the cream to a boil in another medium pan and reduce *it* to 2 cups. The mixture will be soupy unless you really *do* reduce both liquids down to what I say.

Melt the butter in a large heavy saucepan. Add the onion, scallions and garlic and cook over low heat until they have softened and the onion is translucent, about 5 minutes. Do not let the vegetables brown.

Bring a large pot of salted water to a boil and cook the pasta, 10 to 12 minutes.

Meanwhile, stir the reduced cream and stock into the onion mixture, then whisk in the mustard. Keeping the heat low, add the Cheddar, Gouda and Gruyère and whisk gently until the cheeses have melted. Add the seasonings.

(continued)

Check the pasta. Once it's al dente, drain it well. Stir the pasta into the sauce, or vice versa. Spread the mixture in the baking dish, top it with the grated Parmesan, and bake it for 10 to 15 minutes, or until the top has browned.

Serves 6.

Cold "Barbecued" Pork Loin

W HEN YOU READ THIS RECIPE, you may worry that the different
ingredients will never pull together. Rest assured that they do.
The woman who tested this pork had the option of checking
"Delicious," "Good," "Just Okay" or "Bad" on her test report. She crossed
them all off and wrote "*Excellent*"—another good grade for Lucy Dobson.

Cold pork makes a nicely surprising thing to serve guests. Imagine how
their hearts will sink when you tell them they're going to have cold pork
for supper—and then, what relief they'll feel when you bring this out. It's
not really barbecued, but the sweet, spicy sauce is kind of barbecue-ish. A
nice accompaniment is Upgraded Applesauce (page 138).

1	5-pound loin of pork, trimmed of all fat, boned and tied
	Dry mustard and dried thyme to taste
½	cup plus 2 tablespoons dry sherry
½	cup plus 1 tablespoon soy sauce
3	large garlic cloves, finely chopped
3	tablespoons grated fresh ginger
1	8-ounce jar currant jelly (it's okay, you'll like it)

Rub the meat all over with liberal amounts of mustard and thyme and let it sit at
room temperature for 1 hour.

In a small bowl or measuring cup, combine ½ cup each of the dry sherry and soy
sauce. Add the garlic and 2 tablespoons of the grated ginger and pour the marinade over the meat. Chill the meat, covered, for at least 12 hours, turning it often. (You don't have to get up during the night to do it though.)

The next morning, let the meat sit at room temperature for 1 to 2 hours. Preheat
the oven to 325 degrees F. Roast the pork in the marinade for 25 minutes per
pound, basting it frequently. (Let me tell you here that I'm only *saying* 25 minutes a pound because I don't want anyone out there suing me. I myself roast the
meat for 20 minutes a pound. These days, pork doesn't need to be cooked until
it's gray to be safe.)

(continued)

Once the pork is done, put it on a platter, tray—whatever. In a heavy pan, over medium heat, melt the currant jelly. Once it's bubbling, add the remaining 2 tablespoons sherry, the remaining 1 tablespoon soy sauce and the remaining 1 tablespoon grated ginger. Spoon this sauce over the pork.

Let the pork come to room temperature. Don't refrigerate it unless the weather is roasting-hot. Otherwise, there will be the little problem of congealed fat. Obviously, you'll have to refrigerate any leftovers once your guests have gone home.

Serves 6.

"I'm only *saying* 25 minutes a pound because I don't want anyone suing me."

Pot Roast with Leeks and Brandy

My FRIEND LUCY DOBSON is a good person to have lunch with. Not only do you get to see her incredible homemade quilted potholders, you also come away with many great recipes, like this one. Lucy's pot roast perfectly combines the homey texture of pot roast with a rich, multifaceted "company" taste. If you're ever writing a cookbook of your own, be warned that it just won't work out unless Lucy asks you to lunch.

1 4-pound standing rump roast
6 slices thick-cut bacon, cooked until crisp and crumbled
2 garlic cloves, minced
2 teaspoons salt
1 teaspoon dried thyme leaves
¼ teaspoon freshly grated nutmeg
¼ teaspoon ground cloves
1 cup brandy
1 cup dry red wine
4 leeks, cut into 1-inch pieces
4 large carrots, sliced (there's no need to peel them)

Preheat the oven to 350 degrees F.

Place everything except the leek and carrots in a large lidded casserole. Cover the casserole and bake the pot roast for 2½ to 3 hours, turning the meat occasionally. The meat should be tender, and most of the liquid should be gone. (Be careful when you open the oven door. A great gust of brandy fumes will leap out at you.) Add the leek and carrot, cover and bake for another 30 minutes, or until the vegetables are tender.

Put the chunk of meat on a platter, pour the fat off the pan liquid, spoon the vegetables and sauce into a separate bowl, and serve. Noodles with lots of chopped parsley make a good go-along.

Serves 4 to 6.

The Roast Beef

I F YOU ONLY EAT ROAST BEEF once in awhile, don't you dare eat anything but a standing rib roast. Standing rib roast *is* roast beef. It's the cut of beef in which, as the name indicates, the meat is surrounded by ribs. Generally you'll have to order a standing rib roast from a butcher, but it's worth it. The massive bones add a wonderful taste to the meat, as well as making it look all Saxon and baronial when it's on a platter. Standing rib roast makes any other cut of beef look like a washcloth. As long as you're spending all that time, money and effort in the first place, please don't blow it on some lesser, just-as-bad-for-your-heart hunk of meat.

And since you're using the best cut for roast beef, make sure you dress it up in party clothes. This herb-pepper crust could almost be served on its own. (Although children may prefer that you trim off the crust for them. As my three-year-old niece said, "I like the pink, but I hate the *brown*.")

You'll need to coat the beef with the crust 24 to 48 hours ahead, so prepare your schedule and refrigerator accordingly. Also—as long as you *are* spending all this time and money and so on—you will find it helpful to read all about standing rib roasts in *The Joy of Cooking* or some other reference/cookbook. Baking these big cuts of meat is a highly personal matter. You don't want to be disappointed, and I don't want you to be mad at me.

> 1   **4-rib standing roast (about 9 pounds), trimmed of all but ¼-inch layer of fat and with the chine bone removed**
> 3   **large garlic cloves, crushed**
> 2   **tablespoons minced fresh thyme or 1 teaspoon dried**
> 2   **tablespoons freshly ground pepper**
> 1   **tablespoon all-purpose flour**
> 1   **tablespoon unsalted butter, at room temperature**
> 1   **tablespoon packed light brown sugar**
> ½   **teaspoon ground allspice**
>   **Coarse or kosher salt**

As the meat waits in lonely splendor, mix together all the other ingredients, except the salt, in a small bowl. Rub the resulting paste all over the beef; then cover the beef with plastic wrap and put it back in the refrigerator for 1 to 2 days.

On the day you're planning to serve it, bring the meat to room temperature; this will take at least 4 hours.

Preheat the oven to 500 degrees F.

Sprinkle the meat all over with coarse salt. Put the meat, rib side down, into a roasting pan.

Roast the meat for 20 minutes, then lower the heat to 325 degrees F. Continue to cook the meat for 1½ to 2 hours, or until a meat thermometer stuck into the small end reads 120 degrees F. (That's for rare meat, which—as far as I'm concerned—is the only way to eat roast beef.)

Once it's out of the oven, the meat *should* rest for at least 15 minutes before you carve it and *can* rest for up to 45 minutes, covered with foil and set on the back of the stove. The temperature will continue to rise for a few minutes after the meat is taken out of the oven, so it will stay properly hot for some time. I myself always plan to have the roast out of the oven about 40 minutes ahead of serving time.

Now wipe your brow and give the meat to someone else to carve. You've done enough.

Serves 8 to 10.

"Standing rib roast makes any other cut of beef look like a washcloth."

Perfect Salmon

I RENE SAX WAS THE FIRST PERSON I actually knew who became a food writer. One day she was just a really good cook, and then the next day she was out there turning food into a *job*. In everything I've ever done, I've tried to copy her.

"The secret here is definitely the sauce," Renie writes. "I got it from Wayne Nish of March restaurant in New York City, who used to serve it over shrimp; I think it's better with salmon. The perfect meal is salmon with this sauce, pureed acorn squash and either spinach or broccoli rabe blanched, then sautéed with garlic."

The sauce should be made at least 1 day ahead.

Sauce
1   gallon apple cider
4   shallots, chopped
2   tablespoons whole black peppercorns

Salmon
4   salmon steaks, each about 1 inch thick
    Olive oil, salt and freshly ground pepper to taste
    All-purpose flour for dredging

Sauce: Put all the ingredients in a big nonreactive kettle and boil them practically forever—well, at least 4 to 6 hours—until you have about 1 cup of syrupy liquid. Strain the sauce. It doesn't need to be refrigerated if you're only keeping it for a day or two.

Salmon: Preheat your broiler and move the broiler rack as close as possible to the source of heat.

Brush the salmon steaks with a little olive oil and season them with salt and pepper. Sift a little flour over each steak. This will form a crust when the fish is cooked.

Meanwhile, warm the sauce over low heat.

Place the salmon, flour side up, as close to the heat source as possible. (I'm repeating this because it's important.) "I then cook the hell out of it," says Renie. "Maybe 10 minutes. I'm not one of those people who like their fish rare, and somehow, the crust that's formed by the flour-and-oil helps keep the inside moist even when it's cooked through." I agree with Renie, but *you* can cook it to whatever doneness you prefer.

Serve the salmon immediately, with the warmed sauce.

Serves 4.

Shrimp with Feta and Fennel

I'M SURE THERE ARE MANY, MANY CASSEROLES out there that are good enough to serve to company, but this is the only one I ever make. I got the recipe from my friend Sarah Crichton, an excellent cook who makes really hard, labor-intensive things like stuffed grape leaves for 20 people. Or anyway, she made things like that before she had a child. I hope she doesn't now, because now that I have kids, I've turned into such a slob that it will make me feel bad if Sarah's still cooking as complicatedly as she used to.

This does take awhile to put together. But a) it's worth it and b) you can make it ahead. Any leftovers are delicious served cold.

2	tablespoons unsalted butter
1⅓	cups chopped fennel bulb
1	cup chopped onion
2	large garlic cloves, minced
2	28-ounce cans plum tomatoes, well drained and coarsely chopped
¼	cup minced fennel fronds
	Grated rind of 1 lemon
1	3-inch strip of orange rind
	Freshly ground pepper to taste
2	pounds large or medium shrimp, peeled and deveined
¼	cup ouzo (this anise-tasting liqueur is essential, so go out and buy it if you don't have it)
10	ounces feta, cut into ½-inch chunks and rinsed well under running water
¼	cup minced fresh parsley
	Plain cooked rice

Melt 1 tablespoon of the butter in a large skillet. Add the fennel and sauté on medium heat for a few minutes; cover the pan, reduce the heat to low and cook the fennel until it has softened, 3 to 4 minutes. Add the onion and garlic to the pan and cook, uncovered, until the vegetables are soft, about 4 minutes. Don't let the vegetables brown.

Add the tomato, fennel fronds, lemon rind, orange rind and pepper. Don't add salt; the feta will do all the salting for you. Over medium-high heat, cook the mixture for about 30 minutes, stirring frequently, until most of the liquid has evaporated. Transfer all the vegetables to a large casserole, but don't bother washing the skillet.

Melt the remaining 1 tablespoon butter in the skillet and sauté the shrimp, stirring, for 1 to 2 minutes, just until they turn pink. Add the ouzo to the skillet and set it on fire with a match. Shake the pan until the flames die down; add the shrimp and any liquid to the casserole. Cool the contents of the casserole for at least 30 minutes. Gently stir in the feta so as to keep the chunks from breaking up. If you're making this dish a day ahead, stop now. Cover and refrigerate the casserole for up to 24 hours.

Preheat the oven to 400 degrees F. Bake the casserole, uncovered, for 20 to 25 minutes, or just until heated through. If you are cooking it straight from the refrigerator, bake for 30 to 40 minutes, or just until heated through. The cheese should be quite soft, but not completely melted. Do not stir the casserole at any point in the cooking; you want the feta to stay in its discrete chunks, not coat everything.

Sprinkle the minced parsley over the top of the casserole. Serve the casserole with plain rice. If your conscience won't let you serve plain rice to guests, mix the parsley in with the rice instead. But don't let the rice get any more complicated than that.

Serves 4 to 6. (I'd say 4, because people really scarf this down.)

"People really scarf this down."

Do Not Make Any Cheese Soufflé But Lucy Dobson's

Yes, it's retro. Yes, it's gal food. Yes, it's not tremendously healthy. Yet once in awhile you *have* to have cheese soufflé, just as once in awhile you have to have tuna casserole. (Although I don't have the guts to offer a recipe for the latter.) Maybe you're *feeling* retro, or maybe you just want some comfort food. Hey, it's your life!

Now, what's the main problem with cheese soufflé? Besides the fact that it falls, I mean? I put it to you that the main problem is those stupid beaten egg whites. Not only do you have to treat them like the spoiled babies they are, but they also muffle the cheese flavor so terribly! Why bother making orthodox cheese soufflé at all, when all you'll end up with is a sunken pile of baked fluff?

Don't bother. Make this one instead. It rises just like a regular soufflé, it looks just like a regular soufflé—though it's slightly creamier—but it tastes 100 percent better. Thanks, Lucy.

2	teaspoons unsalted butter, softened
6	large eggs
½	cup heavy cream
⅓	cup grated Parmesan
1	teaspoon dry mustard
1	teaspoon freshly ground pepper
½	teaspoon salt
	A few shakes of cayenne
½	pound extra-sharp Cheddar cheese, cut into ½-inch cubes
11	ounces Philadelphia cream cheese, cut into globby 1-inch cubes (one 8-ounce plus one 3-ounce package)

Preheat the oven to 375 degrees F.

Use the butter to grease a 5-cup soufflé dish.

Put the eggs, cream, Parmesan, mustard, pepper, salt and cayenne into a food processor or blender. With the motor running, add the Cheddar, piece by piece. With the motor still running, add the cream cheese, piece by piece. When all the cheese is added, process or blend the mixture for 30 seconds. It will be very thick.

Half-pour, half-scrape the mixture into the prepared dish and bake it for 50 to 60 minutes. Don't peek at it before the 50 minutes are up—unless, of course, you have a glass oven door.

Serves 6.

"Yes it's
retro.
Yes, it's gal
food."

Tortellini with Pistachio Sauce

IN THE DAYS when I found this recipe, it was enough just to say "tortellini." Now that there are so many good fresh (or fresh-*ish*) ones in stores, we need to be a little more specific. Use a tortellini with a not-too-spicy filling; no dried tomatoes, in other words. You don't want the sauce to clash with the filling.

If you can find shelled pistachios in huge containers, use them; shelling the nuts is the only chore in this recipe.

Reading the recipe, by the way, gives no clue about how good it is. But I promise—I *swear!*—you'll love it. It's good on other pastas too.

¾	cup shelled pistachios
5	tablespoons olive oil
2	tablespoons fresh lemon juice
2	large garlic cloves
½	cup heavy cream
½	cup grated Parmesan
1	pound fresh or frozen (not thawed) tortellini
	Chopped pistachios for garnish
	Grated Parmesan for garnish

Unless the pistachios are unsalted, put them in a sieve and rinse off the salt under cold water; dry them well on paper towels.

Heat 1 tablespoon of the oil in a small skillet over medium heat. Add the pistachios and sauté for 2 minutes, stirring constantly. Drain on more paper towels.

In a food processor or blender, puree the nuts, the remaining ¼ cup olive oil, the lemon juice and garlic. Add the cream and Parmesan and process for a few seconds more. Cover the mixture and let it sit. Meanwhile, cook the tortellini in plenty of boiling salted water according to the package directions, 7 to 9 minutes.

Drain the tortellini well. Return them to the pot and toss them with the pistachio sauce. Serve immediately, sprinkling each serving with chopped pistachios and grated cheese.

Serves 4.

Perfected Turkey

IF YOU DON'T SUBSCRIBE to *Cook's Illustrated*, you should. It's a great magazine, full of blind taste tests and cooking tips and searches for the best chocolate cake. *Cook's Illustrated* doesn't waste space on filler essays about Hiking Through Mongolia or The Bannocks of My Celtic Childhood; it only discusses cooking the regular kinds of foods that regular people want to eat.

It was this magazine that taught me the secret of brining turkey (and also shrimp; see page 28). Brining means soaking the meat in salted water for a few hours before roasting it. I know it sounds as though you're turning your turkey into a pickle, but the end result is fantastic: moister and more tender than an unbrined turkey, with each bite nicely seasoned.

So I adapted the magazine's brining technique and took my own roasting method from *Beat This!* and combined them. I don't foresee any need to improve my turkey recipe in the future (although in fairness I should tell you that this recipe is going to be more complicated than, say, heating up a Hungry Man turkey dinner). Right now it's as improved as it can get.

Note that you'll need parchment paper for this recipe. And *lots* of refrigerator space. And a nonaluminum pot or bowl big enough to hold your turkey. And you won't be able to stuff the turkey; you'll have to bake the stuffing separately. But wouldn't you secretly prefer that? You have enough to do already.

Brining Solution

1   **fresh or defrosted turkey (use a big, authoritative cookbook
     if you need help deciding how big a turkey to get)**
2   **pounds salt**
2   **garlic cloves, crushed**
2   **bay leaves**
1   **tablespoon whole black peppercorns**
    Corn oil for brushing the breast

Basting Sauce
½   **cup (1 stick) unsalted butter**
½   **cup turkey or chicken broth**
    Juice from 1 large lemon
2   **tablespoons Worcestershire sauce**

Brining solution: Take the little packet of giblets out of the turkey's tummy. (When a relative of mine made her first turkey, she baked the giblets inside it. "I wasn't going to reach in there!" she said indignantly.) Rinse the turkey in cold water and put it into a nonaluminum pot or bowl large enough to hold it easily.

Pour the salt all over the turkey: rub some into the skin, slather some inside the body cavity, pack some into the neck cavity. When all the salt has been used up, pour enough cold water over the turkey to cover it. Add the garlic, bay leaves and peppercorns to the water, making sure they're evenly distributed. Then cover the pot with its own lid or with foil, and chill the turkey for 4 to 6 hours.

When the time's up, take the turkey out of the pot and rinse it thoroughly—nay, obsessively—under cold running water. Pat it dry, inside and out, with lots and lots of paper towels.

Preheat the oven to 325 degrees F. Place a pie pan filled with water on the oven's lower rack. Refill as needed while the turkey cooks.

Flip the turkey's wings backwards to pin down the neck skin. Tie its legs together. (I always truss poultry with unflavored dental floss.)

Take a huge sheet of parchment paper and fold it several times so that you can line your roasting rack with it, allowing 6 to 8 inches of overhang on each side. Brush the turkey breast with the corn oil. Upend the turkey and place it breast-side down in the roasting pan. Staggering a bit, lug the roasting pan over to the oven and push it inside.

Basting sauce: Time for the basting sauce! In a small saucepan, over low heat, combine the butter, broth, lemon juice and Worcestershire sauce. After the first hour of roasting, you'll be basting the turkey top and bottom with this mixture every 15 minutes or so. About halfway through the baking, you'll be able to start swiping up some pan juices with the basting brush and using them to baste with as well.

> "You won't be able to stuff this turkey. But wouldn't you secretly prefer that?"

Bake the turkey for 15 minutes a pound if it weighs less than 16 pounds. If it weighs more than that, bake it for 12 minutes a pound. Turn it breast side up after 1 hour if it weighs less than 12 pounds, and after 1½ hours if it weighs more. You'll probably need another person to help you do this. Pancake turners are a helpful flipping device, or you can put on clean rubber gloves and turn the turkey over with your hands.

When the turkey is done, a meat thermometer inserted into the leg pit and breast will read 165 degrees F. Leave the turkey covered on the top of the stove for 15 minutes so the meat sets before you carve it. Serve with the plain pan juices, or make them into gravy; it's up to you.

Vegetables and Side Dishes

I BELIEVE IT'S CORRECT to open this section with a British joke about "two veg" and the stale smell of cabbage in bygone halls. Then you remind your readers that it's no longer necessary to cook a vegetable to death—*think crisp-tender!*—that potato doesn't necessarily mean French fries, and that no one serves gelatin salads any more. The food pyramid could also be brought in at this point, to give things less of a period feel.

In conversation, this tradition is reflected in the way so many otherwise modest-seeming people brag, "I pretty much only eat vegetables now," or "There's really nothing as rewarding as growing your own produce." Even if both things were true (and they aren't), saying them is just a form of bragging. —*Yes, it is.* Consider how shameful it would sound if you confessed, "I pretty much only eat candy now," or "There's really nothing as rewarding as buying a six-pack of canned pudding."

Poor vegetables! Why do they invite all these preachy clichés? Why do food writers still feel that they have to *sell* us on vegetables? Aren't we all already sold? Is there any doubt that vegetables taste good?

Obviously there is some doubt, or the writers wouldn't go on and on about them. You never read a newspaper article trying to sell you on desserts, after all. But since there's still the perception that the common man doesn't like vegetables, food writers try too hard when they talk about them. Vegetable prose has become to the 1990s what fish prose was to the '80s, except that it's even more dictatorial. Back then, eating fish was better than eating beef; now, eating vegetables is better than eating *anything* else.

The thing is, vegetables can be sold on their own merits. Even if they tasted terrible, they'd still be worth having around. Why doesn't anyone ever write about how beautiful vegetables are?

Isn't Produce the most appealing aisle in any supermarket? Isn't a salad the prettiest part of any meal? (Not counting coleslaw, of course.) Wouldn't it be worth eating lots more vegetables just so you could bring all those colors and shapes into your house? I mean, look at peppers alone!

Am I only jumping onto the vegetable-prose bandwagon in a different way? Am I just saying, No, but I *really* like vegetables, unlike those people who only *say* they do?

Maybe I am. But I REALLY DO LIKE all the vegetables in this chapter.

Recipes

Cindy's Asparagus Vinaigrette 107

Baked Beans 108

The Best Brussels Sprouts 110

Easter Carrots 111

Gingered Carrot Salad 112

Something to Do with Cherry Tomatoes 113

Green Beans in Tomato Vinaigrette 114

Springtime Pasta Salad 115

Kurt's Potato Salad 117

Cheese-Stuffed Baked Potatoes 119

Party Potatoes 120

A Famous Person's Potatoes 122

CMO's Mashers 123

Rice Salad 124

Champagne Risotto 126

Upgraded Layered Salad 127

Snow Pea Salad 129

Watercress Slaw 130

Hot Polish Salad 131

Worthwhile Winter Squash 132

Jace's Favorite Sweet Potatoes 133

Québecois Vinaigrette 134

This Zucchini Really *Is* Different! 135

Cindy's Asparagus Vinaigrette

CINDY KANE is the friend who directed me toward the lentil soup in *Beat This!* It's entirely because of her that I discovered the greatness of walnut oil, which makes all the difference in this recipe as well as in other salad-oriented foods. (Also, see Waffles, page 58.) To think that walnut oil was always just sitting there in the "oil" section of the store, and I never paid any attention! Too soon oldt, too late schmardt.

1	pound thin asparagus spears, trimmed
6	tablespoons walnut oil
1½	tablespoons fresh lemon juice
2	teaspoons balsamic vinegar
¼	teaspoon salt
¼	teaspoon Dijon mustard
⅛	teaspoon freshly ground pepper

Steam the asparagus until it's just tender. (I usually do it for 5 minutes.) While it's steaming, whisk the remaining vinaigrette ingredients together in a small bowl. As soon as the asparagus is cooked, place it in some kind of flat-bottomed vessel. Pour the vinaigrette over it and combine the two gently. You may not think you need all the vinaigrette, but use it anyway.

Let the asparagus cool to room temperature, turning it often to coat it evenly with the vinaigrette. Serve at room temperature or chilled, draining off any extra vinaigrette before serving.

Serves 4.

Baked Beans

BAKED BEANS are like perennial gardens. There so many variables involved that you can't let yourself think about them or you'll never get started. I'll never have a perennial border—planning one would use up my whole brain—but at least I'm not as scared of baked beans as I used to be. Cutting back on the molasses makes all the difference.

I've used the good stuff from many different recipes, including two my mother gave me. (In one, the beans were called Pecket's Soldier Beans; in the other, they were called "dried pea-beans.") My husband insisted on the barbecue sauce. And, to continue this family thing: Most recipes say to keep the salt pork whole, but my father says his grandmother used to cut it into pieces the size of a domino. What's good enough for Great-Grand-mother Helen is good enough for me. (What *was* good enough for her, I mean.)

1	pound dried navy or white pea beans, washed and picked over to remove any shrivelers or other debris
6	cups water
2	ounces salt pork (the rind-y kind called "fatback," *not* "cured pork for beans")
1	12-ounce bottle beer
1	large onion, cut into large dice
1	large garlic clove, put through a garlic press
¼	cup of your favorite barbecue sauce (my favorite is Gates', from Kansas City)
¼	cup mild molasses
2	tablespoons cider vinegar
1	tablespoon dry mustard
1½	teaspoons salt
½	teaspoon ground ginger
	Pinch of ground cloves
1	bay leaf

The day before you'll be cooking the beans, place them in a bowl, cover them with 6 cups of water and let them soak for at least 12 hours.

The next day, drain the beans. Put them in a large pot, cover them with fresh water and bring the water to a boil. Reduce the heat and simmer the beans, uncovered, for 45 minutes to 1 hour. They won't be tender, but most of their skins will start to pop.

Leaving the rind on, slice the salt pork into 3 or 4 small chunks—domino-sized, if you want my father to like you. Put the chunks into a bowl, cover them with boiling water and let them sit for 5 minutes.

Preheat the oven to 300 degrees F.

In a large bean-pot-type thing with a lid, combine the beans, their cooking liquid, beer, onion, garlic, barbecue sauce, molasses, vinegar, mustard, salt, ginger, cloves and bay leaf. Mix well. Drain the chunks of salt pork and place them at strategic locations throughout the bean mixture. Cover the pot and put it in the oven.

Bake the beans for 5 hours, stirring them every 30 minutes or so. They need to remain covered with liquid as they cook; add more water if necessary to keep them covered.

Remove the cover from the beans. Bake them for 1 hour more, or until they begin to form a crust on top. Use your judgment here, of course; if the crust begins to look like one of those cracked, drought-ridden deserts in an old *National Geographic*, take the beans out.

These beans reheat well, which is a good thing to know if they finish cooking at 11:00 in the morning.

Makes about 2 quarts of beans, enough to serve 6 to 8.

"I'm not
as scared of
baked beans as
I used to be."

The Best Brussels Sprouts

D ON'T BOTHER MAKING ANY JOKES about how the name is an oxymoron. Brussels sprouts can be very good, and they're so darling that I can't resist serving them once in awhile even to people (like my husband) who hate them.

What *can* be off-putting about Brussels sprouts is not their taste (if you like cabbage to the tenth power, anyway)—it's their texture. Unless they're cooked right, they can be dry and mealy. If you keep Brussels sprouts whole, they really need to come into contact with boiling water at some point in their preparation. Steaming them won't work. Fortunately, this recipe—an adaptation of a *New York Times Magazine* adaptation of an Anne Rosenzweig recipe—doesn't keep the sprouts whole. Are they cuter cut into tiny wedges? I can't decide.

3	slices thick-cut bacon, cut crosswise into ¼-inch pieces
¼	cup pine nuts
1¼	pounds (20 ounces) Brussels sprouts, trimmed of outside leaves, stems trimmed, cut into eighths
1	large garlic clove, minced
2-4	tablespoons water
½	cup coarsely grated carrots
1	tablespoon balsamic vinegar
	Salt and freshly ground pepper to taste
2	tablespoons chopped fresh flat-leaf parsley

Put the bacon into a large nonreactive skillet. Over medium heat, cook it until it's nearly done. Add the pine nuts and cook for 3 to 4 minutes, stirring frequently, until the nuts are golden and the bacon is crisp. Do not pour off the fat.

Add the Brussels sprouts, garlic and water to the skillet. Cover and cook over medium heat, shaking the skillet, for 2 to 3 minutes (or until the sprouts are as cooked as you like them). Add more water if necessary. Add the carrot and stir-fry for another 1 to 2 minutes. Stir in the vinegar and cook for 1 to 2 minutes. Season with salt and pepper. Stir in the parsley and serve.

Serves 3 to 4.

Easter Carrots

O F COURSE you don't *have* to serve these at Easter, but they're a great accompaniment to ham if that's what you're having for Easter dinner. And then the association with bunnies and carrots—well, as you can see, I had no real choice about the name. At least I didn't call them "The Easter Bunny's Carrots."

Like most purees, this is ideally prepared 1 day ahead.

- 1 2-inch length of vanilla bean
- ⅔ cup milk
- 2 pounds carrots, pared, cut into chunks and cooked until very tender (I steam them)
- 2 tablespoons unsalted butter
- ½ teaspoon dry mustard
   A few gratings of nutmeg
   Salt and freshly ground pepper to taste

Cut open the section of vanilla bean and scrape as many of its seeds as you can into the milk in a saucepan. Then add the scraped section to the milk as well. Bring the milk to a simmer, stirring, and simmer it for 5 minutes. Fish out the vanilla pod and discard it.

In a food processor, combine the hot milk, carrots, butter, mustard and nutmeg. Process the ingredients until they're as smooth as you like; I like to leave a few chunks for character. Season the mixture to taste. If you refrigerate it, reheat it gently in a double boiler. If you decide to serve it right away, you can heat it in a regular saucepan over very low heat.

Serves 6.

> "At least I didn't call these 'The Easter Bunny's Carrots.'"

Gingered Carrot Salad

THIS SALAD INHABITS A REALM that is far, far closer to heaven than the realm where ordinary carrot salad dwells. You know—the kind with raisins.

In any case, this recipe comes from the Pantry and was created by Lucille Shanks, who has made bathtubs of it over the years. I like gingered carrot salad so much that I can never bring myself to buy any other kind of vegetable at the Pantry except their watercress slaw (page 130).

As with the other Pantry recipes in this book, anyone who lives in my hometown is honor-bound not to try making them; you have to buy them at the Pantry instead. For anyone who lives anywhere else, feel free to make the Pantry recipes as much as you want, but please buy from the Pantry whenever you're in town.

1	12-ounce jar stem ginger in syrup
2	quarts shredded carrots (about 2 pounds)
⅓	cup canola oil
⅓	cup Champagne vinegar
½	teaspoon salt
¼	teaspoon freshly ground pepper (the Pantry uses white pepper)
	Chopped fresh chives as a garnish

In a food processor, puree the ginger, along with its syrup. In a large bowl, mix the carrots and the ginger puree well. In a small bowl, combine the remaining ingredients and then toss them with the carrots. Let the salad sit at room temperature for a couple of hours before serving.

Serves 8 to 10 as a side dish.

Something to Do with Cherry Tomatoes

INSTEAD OF JUST EATING THEM, I mean. Once in awhile it's nice to serve cherry tomatoes hot—especially in winter, when they're often the only worthwhile tomatoes for sale. This is a simple and delicious recipe. You can call them Sherry Cherry Tomatoes if someone asks.

1 **tablespoon unsalted butter**
1 **tablespoon dry sherry**
1 **teaspoon minced fresh dill**
1 **garlic clove, minced**
1 **1-pint basket of cherry tomatoes, hulled**
  Salt and freshly ground pepper to taste

In the top of a double boiler, over medium heat, combine the butter, sherry, dill and garlic. When the butter has melted, stir in the cherry tomatoes. Cover the double boiler and heat the tomatoes for 10 minutes, stirring gently a few times to coat them with the other ingredients. Test a tomato to make sure it's heated through. Season with salt and pepper and serve immediately.

Serves 2 to 3.

Green Beans in Tomato Vinaigrette

FROM TIME TO TIME, you want to serve something salady that isn't actually salad. Or at least I do. I hate to wash salad greens more than almost anything. And don't suggest that one of those salad spinners will make the job more pleasant, because I already have one and it doesn't. Anyway, this is a delicious salad substitute.

1   **pound green beans, trimmed**
2   **tablespoons balsamic vinegar**
1   **tablespoon Dijon mustard**
1   **large garlic clove, minced**
¼   **cup corn oil**
2   **tablespoons *each* minced fresh basil and flat-leaf parsley**
    Salt and freshly ground pepper to taste
1   **pound plum tomatoes, deglopped and chopped**
¼   **cup minced red onion**

Steam the beans for 5 minutes, until they're what everyone seems to call "crisp-tender" these days. Plunge them into cold water to stop the cooking and drain them well.

Put the vinegar, mustard and garlic into a large bowl and whisk them together. Gradually whisk in the oil until you have achieved vinaigrette. Add the basil, parsley and salt and pepper and stir well. Throw in the beans, tomatoes and onion and toss everything together. Serve at room temperature.

Serves 4.

Springtime Pasta Salad

WHAT MAKES THE BEST PASTA SALAD? I mean, how can you go through millions of pasta salad recipes and decide which one is the best? "Put gold in it," says my friend Patty Marx. Or you can just pull out the old recipe you always end up making because, for some reason, it *is* the best pasta salad.

I brought this to an office picnic at my first job a certain number of years ago. (I was an editorial assistant at Chanticleer Press, if you must know.) The women in the office were furious because we *had* to go swimming at the picnic; it was a rule. That's about all I remember, except for this salad and the ninety kabillion manicotti someone else brought.

4	asparagus spears, trimmed
2	small zucchini, about ½ pound
1	cup broccoli, cut into tiny florets
½	cup tiny frozen peas, thawed but not cooked (don't waste your time on fresh unless you grew them yourself; "bought" fresh peas are usually too big and mealy)
½	pound orzo
¼	pound mushrooms, sliced thin
4	medium tomatoes, peeled, deglopped and cut into ½-inch cubes
3	tablespoons *each* minced fresh basil leaves and parsley
1½	cups mayonnaise
2	tablespoons balsamic vinegar
2	garlic cloves, minced
	Salt and freshly ground pepper to taste
½	cup pine nuts, toasted

Cut the asparagus into 1-inch lengths. Cut the zucchini into ½-inch cubes. Steam the asparagus for 1 to 2 minutes; dump the asparagus out of the steamer and steam the zucchini for 2 to 3 minutes; dump out the zucchini and steam the broccoli for 3 to 4 minutes. Everything should still be crisp. If you were lucky enough to find good fresh peas, steam them for 1 minute.

(continued)

Let the vegetables cool while you cook the orzo.

Cook the orzo as directed on the package, about 10 minutes. When it's cooked, drain it and run it briefly under cold running water. (*Never* do this with pasta you're going to be serving hot, by the way; it just makes it flabby and wet.) Drain the orzo thoroughly.

In a large mixing bowl, gently stir together the orzo, cooked vegetables, mushrooms, tomatoes, basil and parsley. In a small bowl, combine the mayonnaise, vinegar and garlic. Add the mayo mixture to the vegetable mixture. Taste for seasoning, adding salt and pepper if you want.

Chill the mixture for at least 4 hours. Re-check the seasoning and stir in the pine nuts just before serving.

Serves 6 to 8.

Kurt's Potato Salad

THIS WAS THE FIRST RECIPE sent to me by a reader—Kurt Anger, of Winnipeg. He obviously knew my tastes—the salad has both bacon and sausage in it. "I have taken a small washbasin of this potato salad to numerous potluck parties, where everyone brought something. I found that my salad was used first and the others were left behind. It tells me that I might have done something right."

You have, Kurt. You have created a potato salad that is BETTER THAN MINE. And here it is.

8	medium-sized red potatoes, boiled in their jackets (Kurt Anger peels them when cool, but I don't think they need it)
	About 3 ounces "garlic ring" sausage (see note), sliced and diced
2	slices thick-cut bacon, diced, cooked until done but not too crispy, and drained well
2	medium tomatoes, deglopped and chopped
2	hard-boiled eggs, chopped
1	medium dill pickle, drained and minced
2	tablespoons minced onion
2	tablespoons minced fresh parsley
1	tablespoon chopped fresh chives or minced scallion tops
	Salt and freshly ground pepper to taste
⅔	cup mayonnaise, plus more if needed
⅓	cup Miracle Whip (see note), plus more if needed

In a large bowl, mix everything together except the mayonnaise and Miracle Whip. Then—yes!—add the mayonnaise and Miracle Whip. Taste for seasonings. If you want the salad moister, add more mayo and Miracle Whip, keeping the same 2:1 proportions. (I use ⅓ cup water instead.) If you want the salad *less* moist, I don't know what to tell you.

Chill the salad for several hours (or up to 3 days), but bring it back to room temperature before you serve it. "Believe me, it tastes better," says Kurt.

Serves 6 to 8.

(continued)

Notes: Readers in the U.S. might have trouble finding garlic ring sausage; I've never found it, myself. As Kurt Anger suggested, I substitute salami and add a small clove of minced garlic. The next time I go to Canada, I'll buy the real thing.

You may be suspicious of the Miracle Whip; I was too. But it's okay—go ahead and use it. Kurt had anticipated our suspicions in his letter. Miracle Whip, he said, "is very important. The recipe needs it because salad dressing has sugar and vinegar in it and provides just the right combination of mayo mix. . . . I know you don't like salad dressing, but would you try it just once?" I did, and he was right.

> "You may be suspicious of the Miracle Whip. I was too."

Cheese-Stuffed Baked Potatoes

THESE ARE MY DAUGHTER'S FAVORITE MAIN COURSE. For several years she has had them on her birthday, along with some of her other favorites: biscuits, red cabbage and white-chocolate truffles from Teuscher in New York. When I was her age, I always picked Howard Johnson's fried chicken and, when I was a little older, sweet-and-sour pork from the Aloha Restaurant. I liked fine dining, you see. When my mother was little, *she* always chose liver and beets, because it was what her brother hated more than anything else.

This recipe is adapted from one in a long-out-of-print book called *The Starving Artist Cookbook*, published by Hallmark. There are some gems in it, including fish dipped in 7-Up and Red-Hot Jell-O Salad. (The "red-hot" part is from those little candy red-hots.) But these potatoes are legitimately good. Stuffed potatoes aren't supposed to be hip.

4	medium potatoes
1	cup grated extra-sharp Cheddar cheese
¼	cup grated Parmesan
½	cup sour cream
¼	cup (½ stick) unsalted butter
½	cup minced onion
2	large garlic cloves, minced
	Salt to taste

Preheat the oven to 400 degrees F. Bake the potatoes for 1 hour, or until done. Leave the oven on after you've taken out the potatoes.

Split the tates in half lengthwise while they're still hot. Carefully scrape the potato part into a large bowl, saving the skins. To the potatoes add the cheeses, sour cream, butter, onion and garlic. Mash everything well and add salt.

Stuff the potato skins and put them back into the oven for 15 to 20 minutes, or until the stuffing is freckled with little brown dots. Serve immediately.

Makes 8 half-potatoes.

Party Potatoes

WILL YOU PLEASE just take my word for it that I know how to make regular potatoes? And that I often do make them? Because I feel that when I give a recipe involving frozen hash browns, I'm sinking pretty low. I'm hurting my reputation in my hometown as well, because I've served these potatoes to people who loved them and had no idea how easy they'd been to make.

On the other hand, we all have to use convenience foods once in awhile. I can remember a time when I was buying cupcake mix for my son's kindergarten class and I ran into my friend Liz in the mix aisle. She gasped and said, "I can't believe *you* buy things like this!" But was I really going to make homemade cupcakes for 21 kindergartners? No way!

Similarly, there are times when I need (okay, *want*) to make a delicious potato dish in quantity—say, to serve 20 or 30 or 40 people. Yes, I could make a rice dish or a pasta dish or something else from a starch that's easy to multiply. But maybe I'm in a potato mood! Maybe I just don't *feel* like peeling and parboiling and cooking up enough potatoes to serve 40 people! Hey, maybe I'm making potatoes for 100 people! *How do you know how many I'm serving?*

This recipe serves 20. (Actually, it was meant to serve 30, but I'm saying it serves 20 because the last time I made this quantity for 20 people, there was nothing left over.) It can be multiplied indefinitely. It can be baked at any old temperature, depending on what else you need your oven for. It tastes wonderful; people will scrape the bottom of the pan, and no one will ever guess your dirty little secret. You should *thank* me for having enough humility to give you this recipe.

3   large bags thawed Ore-Ida Frozen Hashed Browns (the size that contains 11 servings)—or other equivalent weight of frozen shredded or cubed potatoes

3   **very large onions, diced (about 6 cups)**
4   **large garlic cloves, crushed**
1   **tablespoon freshly ground pepper, plus more to taste**
1½-2   **pounds Gruyère, grated**
1½-2   **pounds Havarti, grated**
3-4   **5-ounce containers Boursin with herbs, crumbled**
1   **pint half-and-half**

Preheat the oven to 350 degrees F, or whatever. Grease a large roasting pan.

In a very large (8-to-13-quart) bowl, combine the thawed potatoes, onions, garlic and pepper with your hands, tossing until well combined. Now mix in the smaller quantity of all the cheeses thoroughly. Taste for seasonings, adding more cheeses and more pepper if you want. It's unlikely you'll need salt, with all this cheese. That's why these potatoes are so healthy—no added salt! Pack the tates into the roasting pan, pour the half-and-half over them, and grind some more pepper on top.

Bake the potatoes, uncovered, for at least 1 hour, depending on how crusty you want them to be. I usually bake them for 2 hours, because we like them very brown. Halfway through the baking, stir the potatoes from the bottom up to get the already formed brown bits mixed throughout. Thereafter, leave the potatoes alone. If they're getting brown faster than you want, cover the pan or lower the heat; if you have the opposite problem, turn up the heat. This is a very forgiving recipe.

Serves 20 or more.

"You should *thank* me for having the humility to give you this recipe."

A Famous Person's Potatoes

IN THIS CASE Nora Ephron is the famous person. She is very nice besides; I especially like her because she didn't curl her lip when I mentioned how much candy I eat. Here is her potato recipe, exactly as she gave it to me. If I had known when I was first reading Nora's magazine stuff that one day I would be including a recipe of hers in a cookbook, I would have—well, what *would* I have done?

"I would be happy to send you a recipe for potatoes fried in *grieven*, which you know as onions sautéed in cracklings made from chicken fat. Oh well, I've gone this far I might as well give it to you: You take about ½ pound of unrendered chicken fat. Cut each bit into 3 or 4 smaller pieces. Put it into a large frying pan and as it's starting to melt and get hot, add 1 chopped medium onion. When the onion is golden, add 3 russet potatoes cut into dice and sauté together over slightly more than medium heat until everything is crisp. This can take awhile. Drain on towels. We eat this with roast chicken."

Another, more recherché version is to mail-order rendered duck fat from D'Artagnan in New Jersey. (See Leftovers, page 197.) "Better than butter!" the duck-fat container says on top. And really, it almost *is*.

CMO's Mashers

C MO IS MY MOTHER-IN-LAW, Carol Matz Owen. She is the only person who really understands the human need for bacon. (See her bacon-cooking method in Leftovers, page 196.) In her house, they have it for breakfast *every day*!

Carol also understands mashed potatoes. This recipe is the only do-ahead version that actually tastes as good as freshly made. If you haven't pinned it down for yourself already, here it is. You'll thank Carol every Thanksgiving.

I never boil potatoes when I'm going to mash them. I always bake them: more taste and less work. Using red potatoes—Carol's suggestion—makes for a creamier product. Using baked potatoes instead of boiled means that you'll probably need to add extra liquid to the recipe. After all, those potatoes weren't absorbing moisture as they baked.

9	large red potatoes, just baked
½	cup (1 stick) unsalted butter, softened
12	ounces Philadelphia cream cheese, softened
¾	cup sour cream
	Hot milk if necessary
	Salt and freshly ground pepper
2	tablespoons unsalted butter, melted

Cut the hot potatoes in half and scoop their steaming insides into a large bowl. (I put the scooped-out mixture through a ricer, but this isn't mandatory.) With an electric mixer, beat in the butter, cream cheese and sour cream. If the mixture seems gummy, add hot milk until you reach the texture you want. Season to taste.

You can, of course, serve these immediately. But why, when they'll reheat so beautifully? Instead, pack them into a buttered casserole and pour the melted butter on top. Then let them cool, cover them with foil, and chill for up to 48 hours.

To reheat, bring the potatoes to room temperature (it will take at least 2 hours) and preheat the oven to 300 degrees F. Bake them, uncovered, for 20 to 30 minutes, or until heated through.

Serves 8.

Rice Salad

THIS ISN'T MY RICE SALAD RECIPE. That consists of brown rice, scallions and a tomato-orange mayonnaise that I make by doctoring up Hellman's mayo with tomato paste, lemon juice and lots of grated orange rind. There. Now you have the recipe for *my* rice salad. *This* rice salad is adapted from a tattered old Xerox given to me by my friend Lucy Dobson. It's absolutely delicious; it makes a complete meal served along with some kind of green salad; *and* it contains pepperoni, which will make you seem very cutting-edge and kamikaze-ish in these timid days.

Dressing Part

1½	cups corn oil
¾	cup balsamic vinegar
2	teaspoons freshly ground pepper
1	teaspoon salt
¼	cup *each* minced fresh parsley and fresh basil (you'll be using more parsley later, so mince ½ cup total)
1	tablespoon fresh oregano or ½ teaspoon dried
1	tablespoon minced garlic

Salad Part

6	cups cooked brown or white rice (I prefer brown)
¾	pound cooked peeled shrimp (see page 28), cut into thirds
¼	pound pepperoni, sliced into matchsticks
1	large green bell pepper, finely chopped
1	large red bell pepper, finely chopped
1	cup quartered cooked artichoke hearts
½	cup minced red onion
½	cup dried currants
4	scallions, sliced (include as much green part as possible)
¼	cup minced fresh parsley
2	tablespoons minced fresh dill

Dressing part: Whisk all the ingredients together in a small bowl and set aside.

Salad part: In a large bowl, combine all the salad ingredients, mixing well. Add the dressing gradually, stopping when you think the salad is moist enough. Reserve the remaining dressing. Toss everything until thoroughly combined. Chill the salad for at least 4 hours before serving. Stir in more dressing to taste, if you think the salad needs it.

Serve cold or at room temperature.

Serves 6 to 8.

"This will make you seem very cutting-edge and kamikaze-ish."

Champagne Risotto

IT'S FUNNY: I wouldn't be nearly as embarrassed to give you a recipe for, say, baloney-cream cheese roll-ups as I am to give you something that's only *slightly* dated. I guess it's sort of like the way clothes from 30 years ago look better than clothes from 5 years ago. And to have *champagne* in it—God, that sounds even *more* '80s! The problem is that this recipe, which my sister Cathy sent me a few years ago, is very, very good. You can just call it rice if you're worried about sounding faded. "Wine rice," maybe. That should be un-trendy enough for anyone.

2	tablespoons unsalted butter
1	cup chopped shallots
10	ounces fresh porcini or other wild mushrooms, sliced
2	cups Arborio or other Italian short-grain rice
1	teaspoon dried thyme
½	teaspoon salt
1	cup warm water
3	cups not-too-elegant Champagne
1	cup chopped fresh flat-leaf parsley
1	cup grated Parmesan

In a large pot, over medium heat, melt the butter. Add the shallots and mushrooms and sauté for 5 minutes, until softened. Add the rice, thyme and salt and stir for 1 to 2 minutes. Then keep adding small dollops of water and Champagne, stirring until each addition is absorbed and the rice is cooked. My sister's note adds, "Keep tasting till rice is right consistency." Fine with me! The whole process will take 20 to 30 minutes, so have a book with you.

As soon as the rice *is* "right consistency," stir in the parsley and cheese and serve immediately.

Serves 6 to 8.

Upgraded Layered Salad

REMEMBER WHEN the original layered salad swept all the potlucks? I first tasted it at a bridal shower (I was the bride) at the Warwicks' house in Kansas City. I was so enraptured that I made it every time I turned around, for every possible occasion. Unfortunately, so did everyone else in the country. "We had that layered salad again," I reported glumly to my mother once after a picnic. "Is that the one with the peas?" she said wearily.

So I thought it was time to upgrade the recipe a little. (Even though I left in the peas. I *like* them.) Layered salad is still a great idea, and it *can* be made ahead, and it serves a lot of people, so why shouldn't it be revived in time for the millennium?

You'll need a container that holds 4 quarts. Mary Warwick, who is the original creator of this recipe as far as I'm concerned, suggests a punch bowl. Another suggestion—this one mine, mine, mine: Buy two packs of spinach and pick the best leaves out of each, rather than struggling to make one bag do. All those soft, wet, broken leaves that you try to convince yourself are really okay—wouldn't you rather not deal with them at all?

Salad

1	10-ounce bag fresh spinach, carefully washed and drained
¼	pound mushrooms, sliced thin
1	20-ounce package thick-cut bacon, cooked and crumbled
1	bunch scallions, cut into ¼-inch slices (include as much of the green as possible)
4	large tomatoes, peeled, deglopped and chopped
1	10-ounce package tiny frozen green peas, thawed but not cooked (they must be the tiny kind)
2	cups chopped watercress

Dressing

⅓   cup parsley sprigs, packed
1   garlic clove, peeled
2   tablespoons white-wine vinegar
1   teaspoon Worcestershire sauce
1   cup mayonnaise
1   cup sour cream
½   teaspoon freshly ground pepper

Topping

1   pound Gruyère, grated

Salad: In the aforementioned large bowl or punch bowl, layer the salad ingredients in the order listed, starting with the spinach and ending with the watercress.

Dressing: In a food processor or blender, mince the parsley and garlic with the vinegar and Worcestershire sauce. Add the mayonnaise and re-process until smooth. Scrape this mixture into a small bowl and stir in the sour cream and pepper thoroughly.

Assembly and Topping: "Ice" the salad with the dressing. In other words, spread the dressing across the top of the salad but don't mix it in. It will mix *itself* in, you see. Spread the grated Gruyère evenly across the dressing.

Cover the bowl with foil and chill the salad for 24 hours.

Traditionally, this salad is not tossed before serving; you're supposed to plunge a spoon down to the bottom of the bowl and deftly spoon up one layer of each ingredient. However, my friend Sarah Gaede always tosses *her* layered salad so that all the elements will be mixed. It's your call.

Serves 20.

"Why shouldn't layered salad be revived in time for the millennium?"

Snow Pea Salad

THIS APPROXIMATES a wonderful salad I used to eat at a Japanese restaurant in New York. I always asked for it even when it wasn't on the menu, the one time I've ever been so bold. I ate this salad a lot when I was pregnant, but my daughter, strangely enough, does not appreciate it. Maybe one day she will.

- 1 **pound snow peas, trimmed and de-ended**
- ¼ **cup sesame seeds, toasted**
- 1 **teaspoon Asian sesame oil**
- 3 **tablespoons Japanese soy sauce (you can substitute regular soy sauce)**
- 1 **tablespoon mirin (rice wine) or dry sherry**
- 2 **teaspoons white vinegar**
- 2 **teaspoons sugar**
  A few gratings of fresh ginger

Steam the snow peas for NO MORE THAN 1 MINUTE; then rinse them quickly under cold water and drain them well. Your goal here is to have them seem raw without being obnoxiously so. Toss the drained snow peas with the toasted sesame seeds.

In a medium bowl, combine the other ingredients and toss the snow peas with *them*. Let the salad sit for at least 30 minutes before serving at room temperature—although if you're serving it in the full blaze of summer, you might prefer to chill it for 2 hours and serve it cold.

Serves 4 to 6.

Watercress Slaw

IN THE OLDEN DAYS, when people didn't really like vegetables, the vegetables in coleslaw were heavily disguised—blanched, sugared and covered with white glop. Now that we no longer think of vegetables as animal fodder, it's okay to make coleslaw that actually tastes like its main ingredients. *I* don't have to make this coleslaw; I can buy it at the Pantry, a gourmet shop about two minutes from my house. But here's their recipe so you can make it.

Slaw

1	**2-to-2½-pound cabbage, trimmed of outer leaves**
1	**large bunch watercress, carefully washed and de-stemmed**
1	**large yellow onion**
5	**red radishes, thinly sliced**
⅓	**cup white-wine vinegar**
1	**tablespoon sugar**
	Salt and freshly ground pepper to taste

Dressing

1	**cup good mayonnaise (I use Hellman's)**
¾	**cup sour cream**
¼	**cup heavy cream**
1	**tablespoon horseradish, either freshly grated or bottled (if bottled, drain it well)**

Slaw: Cut the cabbage into thin wedges and remove the core. Chop it in a food processor along with the watercress and onion.

Transfer the mixture to a large serving bowl. Add the radishes, vinegar, sugar and salt and pepper. Mix everything well.

Dressing: In a small bowl, combine the dressing ingredients. Slowly stir the dressing into the vegetables, stopping when you think the slaw is moist enough. Chill the slaw for at least 1 hour before you serve it.

Serves 8.

Hot Polish Salad

That's Poe-lish, not pah-lish. You're not going to be spreading hot polish on your salad. This recipe, from family friend Sue Olson, is my favorite way to do cabbage. It's old-fashioned and comforting and wintry and Teutonic and not at all good for you, but that doesn't matter. Sue sent the recipe to me under the title "Best Everyday Vegetable."

This recipe isn't worth trying unless you're willing to use the bacon fat called for. Well, it's worth *trying*, but you won't like it nearly as much, and neither will I.

½	small head of red cabbage
2	tablespoons bacon fat
2	medium onions, chopped
1	Granny Smith apple, peeled, cored and coarsely chopped
3	tablespoons vinegar (I use balsamic)
2	tablespoons packed light brown sugar
	Salt and freshly ground pepper to taste
1	teaspoon caraway seeds (optional)

Remove the outer leaves and hard core from the cabbage. Chop the leaves coarsely.

Heat the bacon fat in a large nonreactive skillet. Add the onions and sauté over medium heat until they're tender, about 5 minutes. Add the cabbage and stir to blend it well with the onions. Cover the skillet and let the cabbage steam-fry for 10 minutes. Add the apple, vinegar and brown sugar.

Cook the cabbage, stirring frequently, until it's as done as you like. If you asked me how long *I* cook it, I'd say, "About 7 minutes." Season it, stir in the caraway seeds, if you're using them, and serve the cabbage hot or at room temperature.

Serves 4 to 6.

"You're not going to be spreading hot polish on your salad."

Worthwhile Winter Squash

DID YOU EVER get the feeling that all winter squash recipes are identical? Smooth, brown, sweet, reheated-tasting—as though the goal of all those recipes was to make squash fresh from the can. Well, this one stands out from all the rest. It can be made ahead of time, too, but don't hold that against it.

1¼	**pounds butternut or acorn squash, peeled, seeded and cut into thin slices**
3	**tablespoons unsalted butter**
	Salt and freshly ground pepper to taste
	A few gratings of nutmeg
1	**cup heavy cream**
⅓	**cup Madeira**
½	**cup fresh bread crumbs**
½	**cup chopped walnuts**
2	**tablespoons unsalted butter, melted**

Preheat the oven to 325 degrees F.

In a large skillet, sauté the squash in the butter until it begins to brown, 4 to 6 minutes. Stir in the salt, pepper and nutmeg. In a small bowl, stir together the cream and Madeira.

Put half of the seasoned squash into a greased 1-quart baking dish. Over it, pour half of the cream-Madeira mixture. Now do it again with the other two halves.

In a small bowl, stir together the bread crumbs, chopped walnuts and melted butter. Sprinkle them over the squash, making sure you sprinkle the edges. *Someone's* going to be eating squash from the edge of the dish, you know.

Bake the squash for 45 to 50 minutes, or until it's tender and the topping is brown. If you *do* decide to make this ahead, don't bake it. Refrigerate it, then let it sit out at room temperature for 1 hour, and bake it for 1 hour.

Serves 6.

Jace's Favorite Sweet Potatoes

JACE HAESTAD is a friend of my son John's. This recipe comes from a cookbook John and Jace's first-grade class put together at Thanksgiving. It's one of our family's favorites now too. (I've reduced the sugar from the original 6 cups.) The potatoes do have to simmer for a couple of hours, but tell me you won't be hanging around the kitchen for at *least* that long on Thanksgiving Day!

10	large sweet potatoes (about 6 pounds)
4	cups sugar
2½	cups water
1¼	cups strained fresh orange juice
¾	cup strained fresh lime juice
6	tablespoons (¾ stick) unsalted butter

Scrub the sweet potatoes, put them into a large pot and cover them with water. Bring the water to a boil; then cover the pot, reduce the heat to medium-low and simmer the potatoes until they're barely tender enough to be pierced with a fork, about 30 minutes. Drain the potatoes and let them cool. Peel them, removing all the brownish material below the skin. Cut them in half lengthwise.

Combine the sugar, water and juices and divide between 2 large nonreactive skillets or pans big enough to hold the potatoes in a single layer. Bring the liquid to a simmer. Add the potatoes and turn the heat to its lowest setting. Cook the potatoes, turning them gently once in awhile—I use tongs—for about 2 hours, or until they are translucent around the edges.

Melt the butter in a small saucepan. Arrange the potatoes in a serving dish, drizzle them with the butter, and have a happy Thanksgiving.

Makes 20 potato halves.

Québecois Vinaigrette

WOULD YOU BE INTERESTED in a more enticing, complex vinaigrette?" wrote Joe Bontems of Rockburn, Quebec. Yes, Mr. Bontems, I would, as long as you promise to try the cinnamon rolls in *Beat This! Cookbook* sometime. I know they don't sound good, but they *are*.

As with all vinaigrettes, this one's proportions can be varied to suit your taste. As originally written, it actually calls for more vinegar than oil. I prefer it this way, but you can certainly reverse the vinegar/oil ratio if you want something a little milder. The original also calls for white pepper. ("Lots!" Joe Bontems says.) I always use black, myself, so I've just written "pepper."

¼	cup cider vinegar (Joe Bontems uses unpasteurized)
2	tablespoons olive oil
1	tablespoon fresh lemon juice
2	teaspoons Dijon mustard
2	teaspoons chopped fresh chives
2	teaspoons minced fresh thyme or ½ teaspoon dried
1	garlic clove, crushed
½	teaspoon pure maple syrup
	Coarse salt and freshly ground pepper to taste

In a small bowl, whisk everything together until emulsified. Let the vinaigrette rest for at least 1 hour before you serve it, and whisk it again before using.

Makes about ½ cup.

No, This Zucchini Really *Is* Different!

I'M NOT GOING TO MAKE a lot of zucchini jokes here. You know, the ones about how everyone's garden is so full of boat-sized zucchini at the end of the summer that there's nothing to do but smuggle it into *other* people's gardens. Even at summer's end, people would still be happy to be served this recipe.

1 tablespoon unsalted butter
¼ cup dry vermouth
6 small zucchini, thinly sliced
1 large onion, chopped
1 large garlic clove, minced
1 tablespoon minced fresh thyme or 1 teaspoon dried—wouldn't
   it make more sense for you to grow herbs than zucchini?
Salt and freshly ground pepper to taste

Heat the butter and 2 tablespoons of the vermouth in a large nonreactive skillet or large saucepan. Add the zucchini, onion, garlic and thyme.

Cook the mixture over medium heat, stirring often. When the liquid in the skillet is almost gone, add the remaining 2 tablespoons vermouth and turn up the heat to high. Continue to stir and cook the mixture until the zukes are as done as you want them. Taste for seasoning and serve.

Serves 4.

Sauces and Chutneys

THIS SHOULD REALLY BE CALLED "Willie's Chapter." Once, when my son John was about 4, he had his friend Willie Connolly over for pizza. As he always did for John, my husband cut Willie's piece of pizza into small pieces to make it easier to eat. Willie looked at his plate for a long time and finally said, "I can't find the pizza!"

You may have a similar reaction on leafing through this chapter: "I can't find the sauces and chutneys!" There aren't that many of them. I've only just started to dabble in the world of condiments. On the other hand, two of the entries here would have made the *infant* Willie very happy. Let's go back even more years, to the time I asked Willie what he wanted for his second birthday. "Apples," he said. "Applesauce."

Two out of six recipes herein are apple-related. Three are for chutneys, which I've just started to appreciate. And the last is for ginger honey. Is there a common theme here? Not really, except that all six condiments have a tendency to creep across your plate and merge with other foods.

Recipes

Upgraded Applesauce 138

Cranberry Chutney 139

Posy's Chutney 141

Lime Chutney 142

Apple Cider Syrup 144

Ginger Honey 145

Upgraded Applesauce

YOU HAVE PLENTY of applesauce recipes, I'm sure—or at least plenty of places to find one. But this recipe, adapted from Sally and Martin Stone's *Essential Root Vegetable Cookbook*, is different. Though it's still comfort food, it's not *baby* food. Serve it with sausage, potato pancakes, broiled chicken—any place you'd think of serving regular applesauce, as well as a lot of places you *wouldn't* think of serving regular applesauce because it would be too bland.

Which do you hate the most: peeling apples, greasing pans or washing lettuce? It's a tough choice, but peeling apples used to be my least-favorite kitchen chore. Now that I own one of those apple peeler-corer-slicers, I love it, or at least I don't dread it anymore. I got my apple peeler from L.L. Bean, but they're sold in other catalogs as well as in some cooking stores. I guarantee that you'll use 30 percent more apples if you buy one.

8	**Granny Smith apples, peeled, cored and cut into chunks**
1	**large garlic clove, minced**
⅔	**cup chicken broth**
1	**tablespoon cider vinegar**
1	**tablespoon packed light brown sugar**
1	**large yellow onion, diced**
2	**tablespoons unsalted butter**
	Salt and freshly ground pepper to taste

In a large saucepan, combine the apples, garlic, chicken broth, vinegar and brown sugar. Bring the mixture to a boil; reduce to a simmer. Cover the saucepan halfway and cook the mixture over low heat for 15 to 20 minutes, stirring occasionally, until the apples are tender. When the apples are cooked, puree half of the mixture in a food mill or food processor, leaving the other half chunky.

Meanwhile, in a medium skillet over medium heat, sauté the onion in the butter until it begins to brown, about 8 to 10 minutes. Stir in both the apple mixtures, heat them through and season with salt and pepper. Serve at room temperature.

Serves 4 to 6.

Cranberry Chutney

ANKE FRANKLIN was the first person to tell me about cranberry chutney. Actually, she brought me a jar of it that I ate plain, with a spoon. Then, at almost exactly the same second, my mother sent me a recipe for cranberry chutney that my sister Cornelia had discovered a few years before. Why is it that *I* never seem to make these discoveries? Why am I always the last to know? Anyway, I combined Anke's recipe with the one my mother had sent, then fussed with it a little more. Thanks, Anke, Neen and Moom. And thanks to myself, too, I guess.

Stage One

¾	**pound onions, peeled and chopped**
1	**garlic clove, put through a garlic press**
1	**cup water**
¾	**cup packed light brown sugar**
½	**cup white sugar**
1	**tablespoon corn oil**

Stage Two

2	**Granny Smith apples, peeled, cored and chopped**
⅓	**cup balsamic vinegar**
2	**teaspoons salt**
1	**tablespoon grated fresh ginger**
⅛	**teaspoon *each* ground cinnamon, ground cloves and grated nutmeg**
	Grated rind of 2 large oranges

Stage Three

12	**ounces fresh cranberries, picked over**
¾	**cup *each* dried currants and golden raisins**
	Juice of 2 oranges from Stage Two

Stage one: Put the onions, garlic, water, sugars and oil into a large nonreactive heavy pot. Over medium heat, stirring frequently, cook the mixture for 30 minutes, until thickened.

(continued)

"**Why am I always the last to know?**"

Stage two: Add all these ingredients to the onion-sugar mixture. (Save the oranges. You'll need the juice in the next step.) Cook for 30 minutes more over medium heat, stirring frequently. Don't worry about how ugly everything looks at this point; the cranberries will make it nice again. And here they come!

Stage three: Add the cranberries, currants, raisins and orange juice to the pot. Turn the heat to low. Stirring constantly now, cook the mixture until the cranberries have popped, most of the liquid has evaporated and the stuff in the pot *looks* like chutney. This can take anywhere from 15 to 25 minutes, depending on the size of your pot, the ripeness of the berries and just plain luck.

When the chutney is done, pack it into sterilized jars and seal them up. Refrigerated, the chutney will keep indefinitely.

Makes about 1 quart.

You may as well double the recipe and give some away—to me, if you like.

Posy's Chutney

Posy Benedict (creator of Ginger Honey, page 145, and God's Granola, page 21) converted me to this chutney. It's apricot-based, with lots of garlic and toasted pine nuts.

⅔ cup pine nuts
1 pound dried apricots
6 large garlic cloves, coarsely chopped
1 4-inch-long piece fresh ginger, peeled and sliced
1¼ cups red-wine vinegar
1 pound light brown sugar (2¼ packed cups)
¼ teaspoon salt
¼ teaspoon cayenne (or more, or less—it all depends on you)
¾ cup golden raisins
½ cup dried currants

Preheat the oven to 300 degrees F. In a shallow pan, bake the pine nuts for 10 minutes, or until they're golden. Set them aside to cool.

Put the apricots and 4 cups hot water in a large nonreactive pot. Let the apricots steep for 1 hour.

Put the garlic, ginger and ¼ cup of the vinegar in the bowl of a food processor or blender. Process into a smooth paste.

Add the garlic paste and the remaining 1 cup vinegar to the pot of apricots and soaking liquid. Stir in the brown sugar, salt and cayenne. Bring the mixture to a boil over medium heat. Reduce the heat to low and simmer the mixture for 45 minutes, stirring often. The chutney would like to stick to the bottom of the pot and get all burned; don't let it.

Add the raisins and currants to the pot. Stirring frequently, cook for another 30 minutes, or until it's as thick as you like. Remember that it will thicken further as it cools.

Cool the chutney completely before stirring in the pine nuts. Pack it into sterilized jars and store it in the refrigerator.

Makes 1 quart.

Lime Chutney

How fickle I am. In *Beat This!*, I said I didn't like chutneys. Now I do, or at least I like the three in this book. Maybe my next cookbook will have nine chutney recipes.

Lime Chutney is inspired by a Laurie Colwin recipe in *More Home Cooking*. Laurie Colwin is my citrus muse. She used lemons in her chutney; I use limes. Limes have a slightly less hostile-tasting rind than lemons and much less membrane inside, so the chutney doesn't end up flecked with tough, fibrous bits. Using limes means you don't have to remove all the pith—a horrible task if ever there was one.

I need to warn you that this is an unusual chutney—acrid and assertive—and that lots of people just hate it. I love it, though, and so does my mother, who's the chutney expert in my family. But you *must* let the chutney ripen before serving it. For it to be at its best, you should make it at least 1 month before you plan to use it. "After six months of ripening, it enters into another realm, and no words do justice to the flavor," Laurie Colwin wrote. The longer it ripens, the mellower it gets—"mellow" being a relative term, of course. It is best served with plain, rich meats: ham, pork, duck . . .

2½	pounds limes
1	tablespoon salt
1	cup dried currants
4	large garlic cloves, chopped
1	tablespoon grated fresh ginger
½	cup fresh lime juice
½	cup cider vinegar
1	pound light brown sugar (2¼ packed cups)
1	teaspoon ground cardamom
1	teaspoon ground coriander
½	teaspoon cayenne, or to taste
¼	teaspoon ground cloves

Cut the limes into chunks. In 2 or 3 batches, chop the chunks in a food processor. Transfer the chopped limes to a glass or ceramic bowl and stir in the salt. Cover the bowl and refrigerate it overnight.

The next day, put the limes and their liquid into a large nonreactive pot. Add all the rest of the ingredients and stir until the brown sugar has dissolved.

Over low heat, stirring frequently, cook the mixture for about 45 minutes, or until it becomes thick. Remember that it will become even thicker once it's cool, so try to stop cooking before the stuff is a cementlike mass.

Pack the chutney into sterilized jars and store it in the refrigerator. As I said above, you have to hold off eating it until at least 1 month has passed.

Makes about 4 half-pint jars.

"Limes have a slightly less hostile-tasting rind than lemons."

Apple Cider Syrup

I FIRST READ ABOUT CIDER SYRUP—or "boiled cider," as it's sometimes called—in the King Arthur catalog. (See Leftovers, page 199 for more about the King Arthur guys.) Then, once I'd seen it there, I read about it in both Helen Witty's *Fancy Pantry* and Richard Sax's *Classic Home Desserts*. So I guess I was actually the last person on earth to know about it.

Cider syrup is nothing more than cider boiled down to—yes!—a syrup. You wouldn't want it on pancakes, or at least I wouldn't, but it adds a deep, burnished apple taste to apple desserts. You can brush the top crust of an apple pie with it; you can add a dollop to applesauce or apple crisp; you can glaze baked apples with it; you could even, come to think of it, glaze ham with it. For awhile I got a little obsessed with cider syrup, and once I even dreamed that the King Arthur catalog said, "You can't believe how apple-y it makes everything." At least I think it was a dream. I've never found the quote in any of my catalogs.

You can order cider syrup if you want, but it's easy to make your own if you happen to be poking around the kitchen for a couple of hours.

Put a gallon of apple cider, preferably unpasteurized, into a large pot. If you like, add a cinnamon stick and a few gratings of nutmeg or a couple of cloves. Bring the cider to a boil.

Now *boil* it and *boil* it and *boil* it and *boil* it and *boil* it, for way longer than you could have believed was possible. It may take 6 hours, even.

You'll know it's syrup when the gallon of cider has been reduced down to about a pint; the bubbles in the pot start to turn sticky; little drops of hot cider pop out of the pot from time to time; and the liquid in the pot is tea-colored. When the syrup is ready, strain it into a bowl through a cloth-lined sieve. Cool it thoroughly, pour it into a jar and seal the jar tightly. Store the syrup in the refrigerator, where it will keep indefinitely.

I told my husband how much cider had boiled away before I had syrup. "We expect this of the syrup family," he reminded me.

Makes 1 pint.

Ginger Honey

Posy Benedict and I have a long history of making ginger honey for our church's fall bazaar. We like to rhapsodize about how church women have been doing this kind of work since Elizabethan days. One year, though, we got very technological and borrowed a honey-pouring machine from a beekeeper. It squirted boiling honey all over Posy's hand, so we went back to the Elizabethan method of filling the jars with ladles.

You should *always* have a jar of ginger honey around. Add it to marinades. Glaze fruit tarts with it. Stir a dollop into hot tea. Pour it over vanilla ice cream or lemon sorbet. Mix it with mustard and glaze ham; mix it with mustard and soy sauce and glaze chicken or duck. Flavor whipped cream with it for pumpkin pie. Stir it into seltzer and pretend it's home-bottled ginger ale. Go ahead and eat it plain, if you're so inclined.

8   ounces fresh ginger
2   pounds honey (I use the darkest I can find, but any kind works)

Cut any withered bits off the ginger, then cut it into slivers no wider than a quarter. Put the ginger into a food processor and grind it until it's as smooth and un-fibrous a puree as you can get.

Now pour the honey into a large heavy saucepan. To get out the last ½ cup or so, heat the jar in the microwave for 30 seconds; the honey will pour like water. Stir in the ginger. Over low heat, stirring frequently, bring to a boil. Immediately reduce the heat to low and simmer the mixture for 20 minutes, still stirring frequently.

While this is going on, sterilize a couple of jars. Or just wash and sterilize the jar the honey came in, if you're planning to keep it all.

Posy leaves the honey unstrained, but I wuss out by straining it because I think it's prettier that way. So: Line a sieve or strainer with cheesecloth (or a clean piece of cloth) and strain the honey into a bowl, pressing down hard on the mass of ginger to extract the last drops of flavor. Pour the honey into a sterilized jar, cool it and cap it tightly. It will keep indefinitely. Make sure you label the jar "GINGER Honey" to keep timid souls from mistaking it for the regular stuff.

Makes approximately 1 quart.

"Label the jar to keep timid souls from mistaking it for the regular stuff."

Desserts

I USED TO GO OUT TO DINNER with a bunch of friends once a month. One night, when the dessert menus came, someone at the end of the table said, "Yes, Ann. We know you don't share desserts," before I could even open my mouth.

It wasn't quite fair, actually. It's not that I object to sharing dessert (although, come to think of it, I *do* object to sharing dessert). What I object to is people who say, "I don't want anything. I'll just have a bite of yours."

To such people I would like to respond—as my Girl Scout leader used to say about picking wildflowers—"If everyone did that, what would happen?" All my dessert would be gone, that's what! Leave it alone! Eat a bite of your own dessert, why don't you? No one says you *have* to finish it! Why don't you eat a bite and then give the rest away to the other people at the table?

And another thing: people in Chinese restaurants who want to order a bunch of dishes for the table. What if I want my own entrée all for myself? What if I don't want some of your stupid wontons? But I'll leave that discussion for another time. The point is, I take desserts seriously.

I like to imagine that I'm just speaking courageously on behalf of other (cowardly) dessert-lovers. I'll never forget the time I brought a cake somewhere, and two women argued—literally *argued*, with raised voices—over who should get a corner piece. This showed me that I wasn't the only person in the world who hadn't outgrown my sweet tooth.

But that was a long time ago. Maybe I *am* the only dessert person left in the world. Except for my sisters, of course; our main topic of conversation on the phone is, "Have you had any good candy recently?" My sister-in-law Anne also deserves mentioning here.

If Anne and my sisters and I are the only dessert-lovers left, all the more for us. And keep your fork away from our plates.

Recipes

Ingrid's Almond Tart 148

Very Controversial Apple Crisp 150

Updated Apple Pie 151

Laura and Emmy's Blueberry Pie 155

Coffee-Almond Brownies 158

The Best Thing to Do with a Cake Mix, Part I 160

Hodgecakes 162

The Best Thing to Do with a Cake Mix, Part II 164

Schrafft's Authentic Caramel Sauce 166

Drop-Dead Chocolate Cake 168

Thin, Chewy, Buttery
Chocolate Chip Cookies 170

Instant Chocolate Pudding 172

Ginger Crumb Crust 173

Ginger Squares 175

Licorice Ice Cream 177

Grapefruit Gelatin 179

Key Lime Pie 180

Frozen Lemon Pie 182

New Molasses Cookies 183

Aunt Gail's Oatmeal Cookies 185

Perfect Pumpkin Pie 186

Orange Buttermilk Sherbet 188

Belgian Buttercake 189

Ingrid's Almond Tart

THIS GORGEOUS RECIPE is one I've been promising Ingrid McCaffery for about eight years. Well, for the first five years of those eight I promised it to her, anyway. After that, I just slunk away in shamed silence whenever I saw her.

It's not that the recipe is a treasured secret of mine. It's a treasure, all right, but it's fairly ubiquitous in one form or another; I certainly have no claim to it. I wasn't trying to keep it from Ingrid, either. I just never seemed to get around to *giving* it to her. Who can say why? Maybe I wanted to snooker her into buying a copy of this book.

Crust
1	cup all-purpose flour
1	tablespoon sugar
	Pinch of salt
½	cup (1 stick) unsalted butter, chilled and cut into 8 slices
2	tablespoons ice water
½	teaspoon vanilla extract
⅛	teaspoon almond extract

Filling
1	cup sliced blanched almonds
¾	cup superfine sugar (see page 201)
¾	cup heavy cream
1	teaspoon orange-flavored liqueur (such as Grand Marnier or Cointreau)
⅛	teaspoon salt
⅛	teaspoon almond extract

Crust: The crust can be made by hand, but I always use a food processor. Dump the flour, sugar and salt into the food processor. Process them for a couple of seconds. Scatter the butter slices all over the dry ingredients and process them with on-off pulses until the mixture resembles meal. In a small bowl, combine the water and extracts. With the food processor running, pour in the liquids and process just until the dough begins to come together.

Thoroughly butter a 9-inch tart tin with a removable fluted ring. Press the dough into the tin to line it evenly. Chill the shell for 1 hour, during the latter part of which you will be preheating the oven to 400 degrees F, with a rack in the lower third.

Prick the shell all over with a fork. Butter a 12-inch square of foil. Fit it, buttered side down, into the shell, and fill the foil with raw rice or pie weights. Bake the shell for 7 minutes. Carefully lift out the foil and its contents and bake the shell for another 5 to 10 minutes, or until it begins to turn golden. Let it cool on a rack while you mix the filling ingredients. Don't bother turning off the oven.

Filling: In a medium bowl, combine the almonds, sugar, cream, liqueur, salt and almond extract. Let stand for 15 minutes, stirring the almonds several times. Spoon them into the partially baked shell.

Bake the tart in the middle of the oven for 30 to 40 minutes, or until it's brown and caramelized all over. Let it cool thoroughly on a rack before you slip off the removable tart ring. Transfer to a serving plate and cut it into wedges.

Serves 6 to 8.

Very Controversial Apple Crisp

THE CONTROVERSY is that some people in my family prefer the apple crisp in *Beat This!* to the one here. But I'd trust Marialisa Calta with anything. I've never met her, but we've talked on the phone for at least 300 hours in the past year. If Marialisa says this recipe is better—well, at least *she* must think so, and so must the friends she told me about who are always thanking her for having passed it on. So on the chance that many other people, perhaps *everyone*, will prefer this apple crisp to mine, I humbly bow my head and offer it here.

4   generous cups tart apples, peeled, cored and sliced
1   tablespoon fresh lemon juice
1   teaspoon ground cinnamon, mixed with 1 teaspoon sugar
1   cup firmly packed dark brown sugar
¾   cup all-purpose flour
½   cup (1 stick) unsalted butter
⅛   teaspoon salt
    Vanilla ice cream, if serving warm

Preheat the oven to 375 degrees F, with a rack in the middle. Butter a 9-x-5-inch loaf pan.

In a large bowl, toss the apple slices with the lemon juice and cinnamon-sugar. ("How about nutmeg?" I suggested. "I *hate* nutmeg," Marialisa said firmly.) In a small bowl, blend the brown sugar, flour, butter and salt together—first with a pastry blender or 2 knives, and then with your hands.

Put the apple slices in the loaf pan. Press the topping over them. Bake the apple crisp for 1 hour. At that point, says Marialisa, "you get this really dense, chewy, unbelievable candylike topping."

Serve the apple crisp warm (with vanilla ice cream, preferably) or cold. It is also very good when it's chilled for a couple of days; the topping melts down into the apples a bit.

Serves 4 to 6.

Updated Apple Pie

What's the main problem with baked fruit pies? The bottom crust, of course. How do we know this? Because look at all the methods that have been created over the years to keep the bottom crust from getting soggy.

Prebake the crust before you add the filling, some suggest. Add a layer of bread crumbs under the fruit, others opine. Butter the unbaked crust or spread it with beaten egg white, still others aver. Bake the pie on the bottom rack of the oven . . . bake the pie on a preheated cookie sheet . . . bake a pie without any bottom crust at all . . . bake a really tough, impervious bottom crust that nothing can soak through . . .

None of these ideas work if you have a really juicy filling, except for the idea of skipping the bottom crust entirely and just calling your pie a "deep-dish" one. But dammit, I like to serve a pie with *two* crusts. If I'm going to all the trouble to make pie crust in the first place, I want to get credit for it. And I don't want to cut into my pie and discover that the bottom crust has melted away in a sea of juice.

So I've given up and come up with a new method. I can't say it's exactly easier, but it's not really harder, either. At least it's not as hard (for me) as serving a pie with a wet, gummy bottom crust. What I do is bake the bottom crust, the top crust and the filling all separately, and put them together just before I serve the pie.

I wish I had come up with this method in my first book, so I wouldn't have to do all this explaining now. But I didn't. So here is the description of how I would adapt my apple pie from *Beat This!* After that, I would imagine that you'd be able to adapt other fruit pies on your own.

I realize that the following description may look alarmingly detailed. When I was a book editor, I used to send my authors 15-page revision letters, invariably signing off with, "Please don't be alarmed at the length of this letter!" Trust me, though: You've got a lot less work ahead of you than my authors did. Once you've gotten this method down, you'll be able to make a new, improved fruit pie in pretty much the amount of time it took you to make an old, bad one. Which is still a considerable amount of time. *This* time it'll pay off.

Pastry

2½	cups all-purpose flour
2	teaspoons ground cinnamon
¼	teaspoon salt
1	cup (2 sticks) unsalted butter, chilled and cut into 16 slices
¼	cup Crisco
5	tablespoons ice water
1	teaspoon vanilla extract

Filling

3	pounds Granny Smith apples (enough to make 8 cups sliced), peeled, cored and thinly sliced
1	tablespoon fresh lemon juice
½	cup sugar
⅓	cup packed light brown sugar
¼	cup Apple Cider Syrup (page 144), optional
3	tablespoons cornstarch
2	teaspoons ground cinnamon
½	teaspoon freshly grated nutmeg
2	tablespoons unsalted butter, melted
	Milk for brushing the top crust
1	tablespoon sugar, mixed with ½ teaspoon cinnamon
	Whipped cream to hide the "seams" between the top and bottom crust (an optional touch, and only possible if you serve the pie cold)

Pastry: Stir together the dry ingredients. Cut in the butter and Crisco using a pastry blender or 2 knives. When the mixture resembles coarse meal, sprinkle on the ice water and vanilla extract. Gently gather the dough into a ball with a fork. Divide it into sort-of halves. (One half should be a little larger than the other half.) Press each half into a disk about 1 inch thick. Wrap each in plastic wrap and chill for 30 minutes. While they chill, prepare the filling.

Filling and Assembly: Preheat the oven to 350 degrees F, with one rack near the bottom and another near the top. (You never need to cook a pie crust at a high temperature. It makes it shrink and overbrowns it.)

Butter the bottom and sides of a 9-inch pie pan. On a floured rolling surface, roll out the larger "half" of dough until it forms a circle about 12 inches in diameter. (Keep the smaller "half" in the refrigerator.) Line the pie pan with the dough, being careful not to stretch the dough anywhere. Trim and crimp the edge in whatever decorative fashion you choose. Then stick the pie pan in the refrigerator for 15 minutes.

Put the apples in a big bowl and toss with the lemon juice. Add the rest of the ingredients in order; mix well. Transfer the apples to a buttered baking dish big enough to stir them easily. You're going to be baking them in this, then putting them into the baked pie shell. In fact, you can put the apples into the oven right now if you want.

With the apples out of the way, you now have to think about the top crust. This one's going to be baked on a cookie sheet lined with foil or parchment paper. Roll out the second half of dough about ¼ inch thick. Then, using an 8- or 9-inch round cake pan as your tracing guide, cut out a circle of pastry. Cut this circle into 8 evenly sized wedges. Transfer the wedges to the foil- or parchment-lined cookie sheet. Brush them with a pastry brush dipped in milk and sprinkle them with the sugar-cinnamon mixture. Decorating them with little pastry cutouts is a nice touch, if you're the meticulous type.

Ideally, the 2 crusts and the apple filling should be baked at the same time, and I'm assuming that you have a big enough oven for that. If you don't, you can bake the apples separately.

Butter a 12-inch square of foil and lay it, butter side down, in the pastry-lined pie pan. Fill the shell with raw rice, raw beans or other pie weights. Set it on the lower oven rack. Set the dish of apples next to it. Put the cookie sheet with the cut-out pastry wedges on the top oven rack.

Bake everything for 15 minutes. After 15 minutes, stir the apples; carefully lift the foil and the pie weights out of the pie shell; switch the contents of the upper and lower oven racks; and continue to bake the apples and the crusts for 15 more minutes, stirring the apples every 5 to 10 minutes.

(continued)

> "Dammit, I like to serve a pie with two crusts."

After 30 minutes, the apples won't be done yet—they need to bake for at least 45 minutes—but the crusts may be. If they're brown enough to suit you, take them out now. If not, leave them in a little longer, making sure to check them frequently.

Stirring every 5 to 10 minutes, continue to bake the apples until they are thick, golden and bubbling. Don't worry if parts of them have browned a little; the brown bits will taste good. After 45 minutes, check the apples often. When they're thick enough to suit you, take them out.

If you're going to serve the pie hot, carefully transfer the baked apples to the baked pie shell. Arrange the wedges of baked top crust over the apples as decoratively as you can. When you cut the pie, cut around each "top wedge" so that each person you serve will receive a piece of pie that basically resembles a regular piece.

Alternately, you can keep the top wedges separate until you've already cut the pie. Then top each piece with its own perfect wedge. You might want to do this out in the kitchen, where no one can see you and realize that your drive for pie perfection has finally cooked your brain.

If you're serving the pie cold, you can let the apples cool before putting them into the pie shell. That will keep the crust even crisper.

Serves 8.

"Do this out in the kitchen, where no one can see that your drive for pie perfection has cooked your brain."

Laura and Emmy's Blueberry Pie

My DAUGHTER Laura and her friend Emily have done lots of cooking in my kitchen. (It's Laura's kitchen too, of course, although I'm not always wonderful about sharing it.) In one happy accident, they discovered that blueberry pie with some raspberries in it is even greater than regular blueberry pie. What's even *greater* is the fact that the pie will taste best if you use the raspberries straight from the freezer without defrosting them.

Don't let the assembly descriptions scare you off. They take up a lot of space, but they're not difficult. Follow them and finally, after a lifetime of disappointments, you'll be able to serve a blueberry pie with a crisp, flaky bottom crust.

Pastry

2½	cups all-purpose flour
½	teaspoon ground cinnamon
¼	teaspoon salt
	Pinch of freshly grated nutmeg
1	cup (2 sticks) unsalted butter, chilled and cut into 16 pieces
¼	cup Crisco
5	tablespoons ice water
1	teaspoon vanilla extract

Filling

3½	cups fresh blueberries, washed and picked over
1	tablespoon fresh lemon juice
1	cup sugar
2	tablespoons cornstarch
¼	teaspoon salt
⅛	teaspoon freshly grated nutmeg
3	tablespoons unsalted butter, melted
1½	cups frozen *unsweetened* raspberries, the kind in a bag; do not thaw them

Milk and sugar for the top crust

Pastry: In a large bowl, stir together the flour, cinnamon, salt and nutmeg. Cut in the butter and Crisco, using 2 knives, a pastry blender or your fingers. When the mixture resembles coarse meal, sprinkle in the ice water and vanilla extract. Gently gather the dough into a ball with a fork. Divide it into slightly uneven halves; one half should be larger than the other. Press each half into a disk about 1 inch thick. Wrap each disk in plastic wrap and chill for 30 minutes. While they chill, prepare the filling.

Filling and Assembly: Preheat the oven to 350 degrees F, with one rack near the bottom of the oven and the other near the top. Butter the bottom and sides of 2 9-inch pie pans. On a floured rolling surface, roll out the larger half of dough until it forms a circle about 12 inches in diameter. Line a pie pan with the dough, being careful not to stretch the dough. Crimp the edge in whatever decorative fashion you choose. Stick the pie pan in the refrigerator for 15 minutes.

Put the blueberries in a medium bowl and toss with the lemon juice. Add the rest of the ingredients in order; mix well. Transfer the filling to the second buttered pie pan. Cover the filling with a sheet of foil that you've pierced all over with a fork.

Roll out the second half of dough to a thickness of about ¼ inch. Using an 8- or 9-inch round cake pan as your tracing guide, cut out a circle of pastry. Cut this circle into 8 evenly sized wedges. Transfer the wedges to the foil- or parchment-lined cookie sheet. Brush them with a pastry brush dipped in milk and sprinkle them with sugar. Decorate them with little pastry cutouts, if you want.

Ideally, the 2 crusts and the filling should be baked at the same time, if you have a two-rack oven. If you don't, bake the filling separately.

Butter a 12-inch square of foil and lay it, butter side down, in the pastry-lined pie pan. Fill the shell with raw rice, raw beans or other pie weights. Set it on the lower oven rack. Set the dish of blueberry filling next to it. Put the cookie sheet with the cut-out pastry wedges on the top oven rack.

Bake everything for 15 minutes. After 15 minutes, stir the filling; carefully lift the foil and the pie weights out of the pie shell, switch the contents of the upper and lower oven racks, and continue to bake the filling and the crusts for 15 more minutes, stirring the filling every 5 minutes.

"After a lifetime of disappointment, you'll be able to serve a pie with a crisp, flaky bottom crust."

After 30 minutes, the filling won't be done yet—it needs to bake for at least 45 minutes—but the crusts may be. If they're brown enough to suit you, take them out now. If not, leave them in a little longer, making sure to check them frequently.

Stirring every 5 minutes, continue to bake the filling until it's thick and bubbling. After 45 minutes, check the filling often. When it's thick enough to suit you, take it out.

If you're going to serve the pie hot, carefully transfer the baked filling to the baked pie shell. Arrange the wedges of baked top crust over the filling as decoratively as you can. When you cut the pie, cut around each "top wedge" so that each person you serve will receive a piece of pie that basically resembles a regular piece.

Alternately, you can keep the top wedges separate until you've already cut the pie. Then top each piece with its own perfect wedge.

If you're serving the pie cold, you can let the filling cool before putting it into the pie shell. That will keep the crust even crisper.

Serves 8.

Coffee-Almond Brownies?
Coffee-Almond Blondies? Oh, *Whatever*

THERE ARE VERY FEW NON-CHOCOLATE BROWNIES that seem worthwhile to me. This is one of the exceptions. It does have a little bit of chocolate, but only as a flavor-enhancer—not as a dominant chord. These are sort of like macaroons.

1	3-ounce semisweet chocolate bar (preferably Lindt or Tobler), chilled for about 1 hour to facilitate grinding
½	cup (1 stick) unsalted butter, softened
¼	cup almond paste
1	cup sugar
1	large egg
2	tablespoons instant coffee powder
1	tablespoon milk
1	teaspoon vanilla extract
¼	teaspoon salt
1⅓	cups all-purpose flour
½	cup chopped almonds

Preheat the oven to 350 degrees F, with a rack in the middle. Generously butter a 9-inch square pan.

Break up the chilled chocolate bar and grind it in a food processor until it's reduced to bread-crumb-sized pieces. Transfer the chocolate flecks to a large bowl.

In the food processor—which you don't need to wash—process the butter, almond paste and sugar until smoothly melded. This may take longer than you think; almond paste tends to stay clumped. Once the almond mixture is really smooth, add the egg and process everything again.

Dissolve the instant coffee in the milk. (If the coffee is freeze-dried, you may need to heat the milk first. Freeze-dried coffee doesn't like to melt in non-heated liquids.) Add the coffee-milk mixture, vanilla extract and salt to the gunk in the food processor; process a few seconds. Add the flour and process until everything is smooth.

Transfer the batter to the bowl with the chocolate in it. Stir together the batter, the chocolate and the almonds. This is a messy procedure, and I'll turn my back if you just decide to leave the batter in the processor and pulse in the chocolate and almonds. But the brownies will look much better if you can actually see the almond pieces and the flecks of chocolate—so if you take the easy route, don't homogenize the mixture too much. Spread the batter in the pan; it will be stiff.

Bake the mixture for 25 to 30 minutes, or until a toothpick stuck into the center comes out only slightly sticky. Cool the blondies and cut them into squares.

Makes one 9-inch square pan, or 16 to 20 brownies (or blondies).

"There are very few non-chocolate brownies that seem worthwhile to me."

The Best Thing to Do
with a Cake Mix, Part I

I KNOW I SAID in *Beat This!* that no one else's brownie recipes would make it into this book, but in the case of Ashley Farmen's caramel brownies I must make an exception. This recipe appeared in a cookbook put out by the board of my daughter's nursery school. The board had a hard time coming up with a name for the book. Someone suggested "Nursery Nuggets," but my husband, who was the board's co-chairman, thought that sounded too much like dog food. So they ended up calling the book "Family Favorites."

I hope Ashley isn't mad to see that I've made a couple of changes in her recipe. Ash, I *had* to do it. You'll see it was for the best.

1	14-ounce package Kraft caramels
¼	cup plus ⅓ cup heavy cream
1	18½-ounce package German chocolate cake mix
¾	cup (1½ sticks) unsalted butter, melted
1	cup chopped walnuts
6	ounces chocolate chips (I use 6 ounces high-quality semisweet chocolate, cut into chip-sized bits)

Heat the caramels and the ¼ cup heavy cream in the top of a double boiler over simmering water. Stir frequently until they're well mixed.

Preheat the oven to 350 degrees F, with a rack in the middle. Lightly butter a 13-x-9-inch pan.

Combine the cake mix, melted butter and the remaining ⅓ cup heavy cream in a large bowl until well blended. Stir in the chopped nuts. Pat slightly more than half of the mixture into the pan.

Bake it for 6 minutes, take it out of the oven and scatter the chocolate chips evenly over its surface. Pour the caramel mixture over the cake layer and refrigerate the pan until the caramel is hard. This will make it a lot easier to do the next step.

Pat the second half of the German chocolate dough over the now-firm caramel layer. You won't be able to cover all the caramel with all the dough; a marbleized effect is the best you'll be able to do. Bake the brownies for 18 to 20 minutes; a toothpick gingerly inserted into the top layer of the cake will not necessarily come out clean, but the cake should no longer be doughy. Cool them on a rack and cut them into squares. Chill the pan for at least 30 minutes to harden the caramel, and serve the brownies cold, or they'll be too sweet.

Makes one 13-x-9-inch pan, or 36 brownies.

Hodgecakes

Wʜᴇɴ I ᴅᴇᴄɪᴅᴇᴅ that the Layered Brownies in *Beat This! Cookbook* should have an all-chocolate version, I knew what I wanted the new dessert to taste like. A layer of chocolate-flecked tart dough, a layer of chocolate buttercream, a chocolate glaze—that much was easy. Naming the new dessert was harder; I hate thinking up titles. I blush to confess that I came close to calling them "Chocolate Marvels." How awful that would have been! Luckily my husband came up with the right name in time.

I cut these into small squares, like brownies, but eat them with a fork. They don't quite work as finger food.

Crust

2	cups all-purpose flour
⅛	teaspoon salt
4	ounces semisweet chocolate, coarsely chopped
1	cup (2 sticks) unsalted butter, chilled and cut into about 16 slices
1	teaspoon vanilla extract

Filling

3	large eggs, separated
½	cup plus 1 teaspoon sugar (superfine, if possible; see page 201)
2	tablespoons orange juice
4	ounces semisweet chocolate
3	tablespoons strong brewed or instant coffee
½	cup (1 stick) unsalted butter, cut into bits
	Pinch of salt

Glaze

3	ounces semisweet chocolate
3	ounces unsweetened chocolate
¼	cup (½ stick) unsalted butter

Crust: Preheat the oven to 350 degrees F, with a rack in the middle.

In a food processor, grind together the flour, salt and chocolate until the chocolate has turned into tiny flecks of fairly uniform size. The flour will look "tweedy." Scatter the slices of butter evenly over the top of the flour-chocolate mixture, toss in the vanilla extract and process the mixture with on-off pulses until it forms a dough. Press the dough into an ungreased 13-x-9-inch pan and bake it for 30 minutes, or until firmish and browned. Cool the crust thoroughly on a rack.

Filling: In the top of a double boiler or a bowl set over simmering water, beat together the egg yolks, the ½ cup sugar and the orange juice until they are fluffy, tripled in bulk and hot. Remove the double boiler or bowl from the heat and set the top in a pan of ice water. Once again beat the mixture, this time until it has completely cooled and is the texture of a fluffy mayonnaise.

In a saucepan, over very low heat, melt the chocolate with the coffee. Take it off the heat and add the butter, a bit at a time, beating steadily until the mixture is smooth, creamy and cool. Beat together the chocolate and egg mixtures.

In a medium bowl, whip the egg whites with the salt until soft peaks form. Sprinkle in the remaining 1 teaspoon sugar and continue beating until the whites form stiff peaks. Fold the egg whites into the chocolate mixture.

Spread the buttercream over the cooled crust as smoothly as you can. Chill the pan for several hours or overnight.

Glaze: When the buttercream is cold, melt together the glaze ingredients in a small pan over very low heat, stirring occasionally. Pour this glaze over the chocolate buttercream layer in the pan. Moving quickly, tilt the pan back and forth until the buttercream is covered with a thin layer of glaze. Return the pan to the refrigerator and chill the brownies for at least 2 hours. Cut with a sharp knife. Serve chilled.

Makes one 13-x-9-inch pan, or 36 Hodgecakes.

"I came close to calling these 'Chocolate Marvels.' How awful that would have been!"

The Best Thing to Do with a Cake Mix, Part II

SOON AFTER I'D MARRIED AND LEFT HOME, one of my sisters described a wonderful rum cake a friend had baked my family for Christmas. "It was all steeped in rum, and it had a rum glaze—oh, it was the best thing anyone gave us this year," my sister rhapsodized. "Not better than my shortbread," I suggested. "Yes, better than your shortbread," was her calm reply.

I felt pretty scornful when I discovered that the "wonderful" recipe had both pudding mix and cake mix in it. But that was a long time ago, when I was young and competitive. Now I'm old and serene, and I know that using a mix once in awhile isn't a moral failing if the results turn out well. I don't know if I'd give a "mix" cake to someone for Christmas, but I'd sure eat this one in the privacy of my own home.

Cake

1	cup chopped pecans or walnuts, toasted
1	18½-ounce package yellow cake mix
1	3¾-ounce package vanilla instant pudding mix
4	large eggs
¼	cup cold water
½	cup corn oil
½	cup dark rum
1	teaspoon vanilla extract

Glaze

½	cup (1 stick) unsalted butter
¼	cup water
1	cup sugar
½	cup dark rum

Cake: Preheat the oven to 325 degrees F, with a rack in the middle. Grease and flour a 10-inch tube pan or 12-cup Bundt pan. Sprinkle the nuts over the bottom of the pan.

In a medium bowl, mix all the ingredients together and beat until smooth. Pour the batter into the pan.

Bake the cake for 1 hour, or until a toothpick inserted in the center comes out clean. Cool the cake in the pan on a rack for 30 minutes while you make the glaze.

Glaze: Melt the butter over low heat in a medium saucepan. Turn up the heat to medium, stir in the water and sugar and bring the resulting liquid to a boil. Stirring constantly, boil it for 5 minutes. Take it off the heat and stir in the rum.

When the cake has cooled, turn it out of the pan onto a piece of wax paper. Poke holes in the top and sides of the cake with a toothpick—lots of holes, one every inch or so. Drizzle the glaze evenly over top and sides. Repeat this procedure until all the glaze is used up. Let the cake rest for several hours before cutting.

Makes 1 large cake, serving 12 to 16.

"Using a mix once in awhile isn't a moral failing."

Schrafft's Authentic Caramel Sauce

THE AUTHENTICITY OF THIS SAUCE is vouched for by none other than Julia Child, so no *wonder*. She printed the recipe in a 1981 *McCall's* column, having received it from someone who claimed to have worked for Schrafft's. According to Julia, the sauce was the base for Schrafft's even more famous fudge sauce, but I don't care about that. I only care about my *own* fudge sauce recipe in *Beat This!* So I stop with the caramel sauce, and it's a good place to stop.

1½	cups ice water, if you don't have a candy thermometer
⅔	cup sugar
⅔	cup packed dark brown sugar
⅛	teaspoon salt
½	cup light corn syrup
⅓	cup hot water
½	cup plus ⅓ cup heavy cream
½	teaspoon vanilla extract

If you don't have a candy thermometer, put the ice water somewhere you'll be able to grab it easily. You're going to be using it to test the consistency of the sugar syrup.

Butter the bottom and sides of a heavy medium saucepan. Put the sugars and salt in the saucepan. Scrape the corn syrup into the pan; rinse out the measuring cup with the hot water and add it to the pan.

Over medium-low heat, stirring constantly, bring the mixture to a boil. As soon as it boils, turn up the heat to medium-high and cover the saucepan tightly. Boil the mixture for 3 minutes to allow steam to condense on the sides of the pan and wash down any sugar crystals it finds there. Uncover the pan. Stirring often, cook the syrup until it reaches a temperature of 290 degrees F on a candy thermometer, up to 30 minutes. If you don't have one, drop a little dollop of the syrup into the ice water; at 290 degrees, it should separate into hard, brittle threads.

Take the saucepan off the heat and cool for 3 to 4 minutes.

Gradually, in a thin, steady stream, add the ½ cup of heavy cream to the syrup. If the syrup mixture stiffens, don't worry. As you heat it with the cream, it will dissolve. Return the saucepan to the heat. Cook the syrup to a temperature of 250 degrees; a little syrup dropped into the ice water will form a ball that is firm but moldable with the fingers and will stick to the teeth if you bite it. Be sure the ball has cooled before you try this.

Once again, take the pan off the heat and cool it for several minutes. Stir in the remaining ⅓ cup of cream. Stirring constantly, bring the sauce to a rolling boil without covering the pan. Take the pan off the heat the instant it reaches a full boil. Cool for 1 minute, and then stir in the vanilla extract.

As the sauce cools, stir it from time to time so it won't get lumpy. The sauce is best served lukewarm. Store it in the refrigerator in a covered jar, and reheat it by heating the opened jar in enough boiling water to come halfway up its sides.

Makes about 1½ cups.

Another Drop-Dead Chocolate Cake

I HAVE TO GIVE YOU *just one more* chocolate cake recipe. This one's ratio of chocolate to other ingredients is about 5,000 to 1. I was glad to have it in the freezer when I had unexpected guests. They didn't drop in unannounced; I forgot they were coming. It's basically my (exalted) brownie recipe baked in a cake pan and covered with a very rich, easy glaze. People don't taste it and sneer, "Hmm, tastes like a brownie." They always think it's a cake unto itself.

You will need to use a good brand of semisweet chocolate to make this worthwhile. Lindt and Tobler are both good and readily available. The cake should be made at least 6 hours ahead of time, or it will be hard to slice.

Cake

6	ounces semisweet chocolate
2	ounces unsweetened chocolate
½	cup (1 stick) unsalted butter
2	large eggs
1	cup sugar
¼	teaspoon salt
¼	cup all-purpose flour
1	teaspoon vanilla extract
1	cup miniature chocolate chips (optional)

Glaze

2	ounces semisweet chocolate
2	ounces unsweetened chocolate
¼	cup (½ stick) unsalted butter

Cake: Preheat the oven to 375 degrees F, with a rack in the middle.

Butter and flour a 9-inch round cake pan. Line it with a circle of parchment or wax paper cut to fit, and grease and flour the paper.

In the top of a double boiler, over simmering water, melt the chocolates and the butter. Let them cool to lukewarm (this is important) while you attend to the next step.

In a large bowl, with an electric mixer, beat together the eggs, sugar and salt for 15 minutes.

Fold the chocolate mixture gently into the egg-sugar mixture. Fold in the flour, then the vanilla extract and finally the optional miniature chocolate chips. Scrape the mixture into the pan.

Bake it for 20 minutes.

Cool the cake completely in the pan on a rack. Turn it out onto the rack. Line the serving dish you'll be using with four 3-inch-wide strips of wax paper on which the cake will rest while you glaze it. Make sure the wax paper extends out around the rim of the dish so the glaze won't get all over the dish. Transfer the cake carefully to the serving dish.

Glaze: In the top of a double boiler, over simmering water, melt together the chocolates and the butter. Stir them frequently. When they've melted, remove the top of the double boiler from the heat. Let the glaze cool for 2 or 3 minutes; pour it over the cake.

Let the cake stand for at least 6 hours at room temperature. Then gently attempt to pull the wax paper strips out from under it. If the hardened glaze glues them on, slice away the extra glaze with a sharp knife before pulling out the wax paper.

Use a sharp knife to cut the cake as well. Give people small slices; this is seriously dense.

Serves 8 to 10.

"This cake's ratio of chocolate to other ingredients is about 5,000 to 1."

Thin, Chewy, Buttery Chocolate Chip Cookies

I KNOW THAT THE CHOCOLATE CHIP COOKIE RECIPE in *Beat This!* is perfect as is. I would never dream of replacing it. The thing is, though, that sometimes even I, maker of the world's best chocolate chip cookies, crave the other kind of best chocolate chip cookies. The thin, flat, runny kind. The chewy, foldable kind. To put it in crass commercial terms, the David's Cookies kind as opposed to the Mrs. Field's kind.

This is *that* kind. It's not the David's Cookies recipe, which I've never been able to duplicate. (No one has succeeded, as far as I know.) But it's thin, chewy and foldable. Lots of butter is one secret; the corn syrup is another. Using chopped imported semisweet chocolate helps too. The optional walnut oil, which I'm only making optional so as not to scare you off the recipe entirely—it's easy to find walnut oil in the oil-and-vinegar section of any supermarket—adds a lovely nutty richness without adding actual nuts. I don't like nuts in chocolate chip cookies.

2	cups plus 2 tablespoons all-purpose flour
¾	teaspoon baking soda
¼	teaspoon salt
1	cup (2 sticks) unsalted butter, softened
1⅔	cups packed light brown sugar
2	tablespoons light corn syrup
2	large eggs, at room temperature
2	teaspoons vanilla extract
2	teaspoons walnut oil (optional, but not really)
4	3-ounce Lindt Excellence or other bittersweet chocolate bars, coarsely chopped

In a small bowl, stir together the flour, baking soda and salt.

In a large bowl, cream the butter and brown sugar. Add the corn syrup, eggs, vanilla extract and optional walnut oil; mix well. Stir the dry ingredients into the butter mixture, then beat at medium speed with an electric mixer until you have a smooth dough. Stir in the chocolate chunks by hand.

Chill the batter for 30 minutes. After about 20 minutes, preheat the oven to 350 degrees F, with a rack in the middle.

Line cookie sheets with parchment paper or you'll be sorry. With clean hands, mold the dough into 1-inch balls and space them at 3-inch intervals on the cookie sheets.

Bake the cookies for 10 to 12 minutes, or until they're brown around the edges and golden in the center. Let them cool on the parchment paper before you take them off. I slide each cookie-covered sheet of parchment paper off the cookie sheet onto my counter and let the sheets cool there, freeing the cookie sheet for more parchment paper and cookies.

Makes 4 dozen flat, foldable cookies.

Instant Chocolate Pudding

D ON'T WORRY. It's not what you think. This is a recipe originally published by Nestlé and meant to showcase their chocolate chips. They called it Chocolate Mousse. But instead of being foamy and light like a mousse, it's creamy, dense and unctuous, like chocolate pudding. In other words, it's the best chocolate pudding you'll ever eat. And it takes even less time than the pale-brown scum-topped stuff you make from a box.

You'll need either a blender or food processor for this.

> "This takes even less time than the pale-brown scum-topped stuff from the box."

12	ounces semisweet chocolate, chopped into chip-sized bits
½	cup sugar
3	large eggs
1	tablespoon rum (optional)
1	teaspoon vanilla extract
	Pinch of salt
1	cup boiling milk
	Whipped cream for topping (optional)

Into the blender or food processor, place the chocolate, sugar, eggs, the optional rum, vanilla extract and salt. Pour the boiling milk over all and blend or process the mixture for 1 minute.

Pour the liquid pudding into 8 small serving dishes. Chill for at least 1 hour. Serve, if you want, with whipped cream.

Serves 8.

Ginger Crumb Crust

SINCE THREE PIES IN THIS BOOK USE THIS RECIPE, I'm giving it its own entry. I had a lot of fun experimenting with this crust and am pleased with the results. You can use any gingersnaps you like, even store gingersnaps in a box; the candied ginger will redeem them.

In any case, it's time to reassess crumb crusts. Why do people look down on them when they actually have more personality than most conventional pie crusts? If you're going to be making a pie crust with all vegetable shortening and no butter, the way lots of people do, why is that more respectable than something with some taste and texture? I wouldn't buy a premade crumb crust in the store, but I have no compunctions about making my own. Well, I guess I have compunctions, since I'm going to all this trouble to explain myself; but I'm going to keep using crumb crusts anyway.

1¼   **cups gingersnap crumbs**
3   **ounces sliced crystallized ginger**
2   **tablespoons sugar**
½   **teaspoon ground ginger**
2   **tablespoons unsalted butter, melted**

Preheat the oven to 350 degrees F, with a rack in the middle.

In a food processor, process the crumbs, crystallized ginger, sugar and ground ginger until they're as fine as possible. Transfer the mixture to a bowl and add the melted butter. Set aside ¼ cup of the crumb mixture for decorating the top of the pie. (You don't need to do this if you're using this crust for Perfect Pumpkin Pie, page 186.)

Press the rest of the crumb mixture over the bottom and up the sides of a greased 9-inch deep pie pan. (A greased 8-inch springform pan gives a nicer-looking result for the Frozen Lemon Pie, page 182.) Bake the crust for 10 minutes. On a separate pan or sheet of foil, at the same time, bake the ¼ cup of crumbs.

Cool the pie shell completely before putting in a cold filling. If the extra crumbs need to be crumbled, crumble them. I usually sprinkle them around the edge of the pie, but you can make them into a nice little face or do whatever else you like.

Makes one deep 9-inch pie shell or 8-inch springform crust.

"Why do people look down on crumb crusts when they have more personality than most conventional crusts?"

Ginger Squares

I REALIZE THAT I'VE INCLUDED a lot of ginger recipes in this book. But ginger is the black pepper of the '90s—just as black pepper was the ketchup of the '80s—and I'm as susceptible to trends as everyone else.

Ginger squares look quite a lot like butterscotch brownies, so people will think they're ordinary until they taste them. You can maximize the surprise factor by serving them on a mixed platter of other bars and cookies, or you can warn your guests. It's up to you.

Squares
- ¼ cup (½ stick) unsalted butter
- 1 cup packed light brown sugar
- 1 large egg
- 1 teaspoon vanilla extract
- ¾ cup all-purpose flour
- 3 ounces crystallized ginger slices
- 1 teaspoon baking powder
- 1 teaspoon ground ginger
- ½ teaspoon salt

Glaze
- 2 tablespoons fresh lemon juice
- ½ cup confectioners' sugar

Squares: Preheat the oven to 350 degrees F, with a rack in the middle. Butter a 9-inch square pan.

In a medium saucepan, over low heat, melt the butter. With the heat still on, stir in the brown sugar until it's dissolved. Remove the mixture from the heat. When it is cool, beat in the egg and the vanilla extract.

Combine the flour, ginger slices, baking powder, ground ginger and salt in a food processor. Process the ingredients until the ginger slices are the size of bread crumbs. Stir the flour-ginger mixture into the butter-sugar mixture. When they are well combined, scrape the batter into the pan.

(continued)

Bake the ginger squares for 20 to 25 minutes. The edges should be slightly bubbled and glazed-looking, and there will be a tissue-thin layer on top of the (baked) batter.

Glaze: While the squares are baking, stir together the lemon juice and confectioners' sugar. As soon as the ginger squares come out of the oven, spread the glaze over them. Cut into squares when cool.

Makes one 9-inch-square pan, or 16 to 20 squares.

"Ginger is
the black
pepper of the
'90s."

Licorice Ice Cream

I F YOU DON'T LIKE LICORICE, this probably isn't the recipe for you. If you do, you'll wonder why no one's ever served it to you before. Licorice and cream are an absolutely perfect combination, at *least* as good as peaches and cream.

It can't be denied, though, that licorice ice cream is an odd color—a pale gray-green that more of us associate with Colonial wall paint than with dessert. I feel that this is an advantage, though. It's good to serve people intimidating food once in awhile. It makes them remember you.

You'll need to start the recipe the day before you plan to serve it. You'll also need an ice-cream maker.

1	7.05-ounce box Callard & Bowser Licorice Toffees (or two 3.5-ounce packs)
3	cups heavy cream
1	cup whole milk
4	large eggs
½	cup sugar
1	shake of salt
1	tablespoon ouzo, Pernod or other anise-flavored liqueur (optional)

At least 12 hours before you plan to serve the ice cream, put the candies in a medium bowl with the cream and milk. Cover the mixture and chill it overnight, stirring it once in awhile if you remember. Most of the candies will dissolve overnight; the last bits will dissolve during cooking the next day.

The next day, beat the eggs, sugar and salt together in a large bowl. Pour the licorice-cream mixture into a medium saucepan. Heat over medium heat until small bubbles appear around the edge of the pan. Whisk the licorice-cream mixture very gradually into the egg-sugar mixture. You want to combine the two thoroughly, but not make them foamy.

Transfer the custard—for it *is* a custard now!—to a clean, medium saucepan. Over very low heat, and stirring constantly, cook the custard for 6 to 8 minutes. (A candy thermometer dipped into the custard will read 170 to 180 degrees F.) Cool the custard, then chill it thoroughly. I do this by carefully placing the saucepan into a larger pan of ice and water and stirring until the mixture is cold, about 20 minutes. If you use the fridge, it will take several hours to chill the mixture completely. Once it's fully chilled, add the optional ouzo or Pernod.

Transfer the chilled custard to an ice cream maker and freeze it according to the manufacturer's directions. Transfer the finished ice cream to a sealed container. Leave it in the (regular) freezer for several hours to mellow the flavor and firm the texture.

Makes 1 quart.

"It's good to serve people intimidating food once in awhile."

Grapefruit Gelatin

THIS IS ONE OF THE WORLD'S BEST THINGS to serve at a brunch. I remember serving it to some friends and explaining, "It's kind of like grapefruit Jell-O." The wife turned to her husband and repeated, "It's kind of like grapefruit Jell-O."

It *is* kind of like grapefruit Jell-O, but much, much better. The flavor is lively, the texture is tender—oh, it's just perfect.

½	cup sugar
2	envelopes unflavored gelatin
1½	cups water
2-3	large grapefruits
¼	cup fresh lemon juice
1-2	drops red food coloring (optional, though I use it)

Combine the sugar and gelatin in a large nonreactive saucepan. Gradually stir in the water.

With a vegetable peeler, remove the rind from 2 of the grapefruits and add it to the saucepan. Squeeze the grapefruits; you need 2 cups of juice. Add the grapefruit juice and the lemon juice to the saucepan.

Over low heat, stirring constantly, cook the mixture in the saucepan until it simmers and clarifies. This will take at least 5 minutes. When the liquid is clear, strain it into a serving bowl, pressing down hard on the solids in the strainer so as to get the last drops of citrus elixir. Stir in the optional red food coloring, which will give the gelatin a gentle pinkish glow instead of a bleak yellowish pallor.

If you want, the gelatin can be presented in 4 to 6 serving dishes. In that case, strain the liquid into a large bowl, color it if you want, and then carefully pour it into the smaller dishes.

Chill the gelatin for several hours or overnight.

Makes about 4 cups, serving 6 to 8.

Key Lime Pie

Look! You can order bottled key lime juice for pies!" I once said to my husband as I pored over a catalog. With conversational nuggets like that, it's no wonder David finds me so fascinating. He did look up from his magazine, though. "I can't believe *any* kind of bottled lime juice could be better than fresh lime juice," he said.

Good point! I gave up worrying about tracking down bottled Key lime juice right away, and instead devoted myself to perfecting Key lime pie with the nice ordinary limes I could buy in the supermarket.

One's main task in a good Key lime pie is obliterating the chalky taste of the sweetened condensed milk that provides the filling's thickener. Using a gingersnap crust rather than a graham cracker one is helpful, and so is using more lime juice than most recipes call for. Chilling the pie for 24 hours helps, too, but the filling won't look as nice; *you* decide.

> "Citric acid is nothing but pure, earsplitting sourness."

I also add a jolt of citric acid, which is usually sold under the name "sour salt" or "citrus salt." Citric acid, which is derived from lemons, is nothing but pure, earsplitting sourness, and it's useful for making the filling more tart without thinning it. You can find it in some pharmacies or in the "pickling" section of some large supermarkets. Or get Aunt Gail to give it to you, as I did.

1	baked Ginger Crumb Crust (page 173)
2	14- or 15-ounce cans sweetened condensed milk
2	tablespoons grated lime zest
1⅓	cups fresh lime juice (6-7 limes)
2	large egg yolks, beaten
¼	teaspoon salt
¼	teaspoon citric acid (optional, but well worth it)
1	cup heavy cream
2	tablespoons sugar, preferably superfine (see page 201)
	Grated lime rind for decoration (optional)

Prepare the Ginger Crumb Crust.

In a medium bowl, stir together the condensed milk, lime zest and juice, egg yolks, salt and optional citric acid. When these ingredients are thoroughly combined and smooth, pour them into the baked crust. Chill the pie for 4 to 24 hours.

Whip the heavy cream until it forms soft peaks. Gradually add the sugar and continue whipping until the cream forms stiff peaks. Spread the whipped cream decoratively over the pie filling, sprinkle the optional lime rind over the cream and serve the pie as soon as possible. It doesn't cut very neatly, but no one will care.

Makes one 9-inch pie or 8-inch tart, serving 8.

The Last Word in Frozen Lemon Pies

THIS IS THE ONLY VERSION ALLOWED.

1⅓	cups superfine sugar (see page 201)
2⅔	cups heavy cream
	Grated rind and juice of 4 lemons
	Pinch of salt
1	Ginger Crumb Crust, baked in an 8-inch springform or 9-inch pie pan (page 173), plus Ginger Crumbs for decorating the top of the pie
	Shredded lemon rind for topping (optional)

In a medium bowl, stir together the sugar, cream, lemon rind and juice and salt until the sugar has dissolved. Pour the mixture into the cooled crust and freeze for several hours or overnight. Sprinkle the top of the pie with the reserved crumbs before serving. I like to sprinkle them around the edge, but you can, of course, do whatever you like. Little shreds of lemon rind make a nice topping too.

Makes one 8-inch or 9-inch pie, serving 8.

New Molasses Cookies

TWO READERS HAVE MADE SUGGESTIONS that have greatly improved Grandma Joyce's recipe from the version in *Beat This!* First, John Gregg pointed out that the cookies would be a lot better with more spices. Actually, he said, my recipe was "way too wimpy on the spices. I always triple the ginger, cinnamon and cloves and still wind up with a pretty innocuous cookie."

Second, Frances Manos alerted me to the value of using lard in cookies. This second suggestion may be harder for people to swallow, but only figuratively. Replacing the butter in these cookies with lard *vastly* improves the texture. Bite one, and it twinkles in your mouth.

I hate the thought of lard, I hate the smell of it, I hate the feel of it on my fingers. And yet I won't make these cookies again without it. They're just too much better.

To paraphrase another reader, "I know you hate lard, but won't you please give these a try?"

1¼	cups lard, at room temperature
2	cups sugar
2	large eggs
½	cup light or medium molasses
4	cups all-purpose flour
4	teaspoons baking soda
½	teaspoon salt
2	tablespoons ground cinnamon
2	tablespoons ground ginger
1	tablespoon ground cloves
½	teaspoon freshly grated nutmeg
	Demerara or other large-crystal sugar

In a large bowl, cream the lard with the sugar. Add the eggs and molasses and blend well. In a separate bowl, sift together the flour, baking soda, salt and spices;

beat them into the molasses mixture. Cover the dough with plastic wrap and chill it for 1 hour or overnight. (Chilling it overnight makes for even nicer-shaped cookies.)

About 15 minutes before you are ready to bake, preheat the oven to 375 degrees F, with a rack in the middle.

Line cookie sheets with parchment paper. Roll the dough into 1-inch balls and dip each ball in the sugar. Place the balls 2 inches apart on the cookie sheets.

Bake for 10 to 12 minutes, or until the outsides of the cookies are crackly-looking and the insides are still soft. It's easiest just to slide the parchment paper right off the sheets onto your kitchen counters, but you can also transfer the cookies to racks and reuse the parchment.

Makes 5 dozen cookies.

"I know you hate lard, but won't you please give these a try?"

Aunt Gail's Oatmeal Cookies

MY AUNT GAIL has the sweetest sweet tooth in our family. When I was little, one thing I loved about her house was a chicken-shaped candy dish that always had mints in it. That was before I knew to look into her freezer, where she always keeps about 15 different kinds of Häagen-Dazs and homemade truffles. There are candy bars in her pantry too.

Like my chocolate chip cookies, the oatmeal cookies in the first *Beat This!* are perfect. But Aunt Gail's recipe is for a whole other kind of cookie. Thin and dainty, these would be much more at home at a tea party than the fist-sized monsters I usually bake.

1	**cup (2 sticks) unsalted butter**
1	**cup sugar, plus more for topping**
1	**teaspoon vanilla extract**
¼	**teaspoon almond extract**
1	**cup all-purpose flour**
¾	**teaspoon baking soda**
¼	**teaspoon salt**
1	**cup old-fashioned rolled oats**

Preheat the oven to 350 degrees F, with a rack in the middle. Butter cookie sheets or line them with parchment paper.

In a large bowl, with an electric mixer, cream the butter and sugar together. When they're light and fluffy, add the vanilla and almond extracts. In a small bowl, stir together the flour, baking soda and salt; beat them into the butter-sugar mixture. Beat in the rolled oats with the mixer.

Roll the dough into 1-inch balls and place them 3 inches apart on the cookie sheets; they spread. Dip the bottom of a glass first in water and then in sugar, and then use it to flatten each cookie, repeating the water-sugar process as needed.

Bake the cookies for 8 to 10 minutes, or until slightly browned. Cool them on paper-towel-lined racks and store airtight.

Makes 3 to 4 dozen cookies.

Perfect Pumpkin Pie

PUMPKIN PIE was one of the first things I was going to include in *Beat This!* I kept putting off testing it, though, and then I finally told myself that no one really cares about pumpkin pie anyway.

Unfortunately, lots of people do care about pumpkin pie, so I couldn't escape it this time around. I wasn't worried about the filling. All you have to do with pumpkin pie filling is add a little rum and a lot more spices than most recipes call for. What bothered me was the crust: Is there *any* way to keep it from turning mushy while the pie bakes?

After all, you can't bake the filling separately the way you can for a fruit pie. (See Updated Apple Pie, page 151.) Well, you *could* bake the filling separately if you were confident that you could keep it whole while deftly flipping it out of its pie pan and into the baked shell. Failing that, what are we to do?

A woman I met suggested lining the shell with a mixture of butter and brown sugar, then baking it until the butter and sugar form a glaze. But pumpkin pie is filling enough already. It hardly needs fattening up. *Cook's Illustrated* magazine suggests heating the filling before you put it into the shell. This means that once it's in the oven, the filling will solidify faster. That's true, but it still doesn't completely protect the pie shell. Nor does prebaking the shell help much. Pumpkin filling has an uncanny ability to turn pie crust into mush.

However, using my Ginger Crumb Crust *and* prebaking it *and* replacing some of the sugar with corn syrup *and* preheating the pie filling—combining all four techniques does work. The crust won't be crisp, but it will hold its shape. And Ginger Crumb Crust goes perfectly with pumpkin. Add a little whipped cream—or a big blob of it—and you're all set.

After filling my pie shell, I always have a little bit of pumpkin filling left over. I don't have a 10-inch pan, so I can't use that. Rather than trying to force the filling into the shell and ending up with a nice black layer of pumpkin all over the bottom of my oven, I bake the extra in a couple of custard cups. I put them in with the pie and take them out after 30 minutes. They're nice for breakfast the morning after Thanksgiving, if you're up early enough to eat them before anyone else sees them.

I should say that this is extremely spicy. Cut back on the spices if you're a feeb—I mean, if you like a milder pie.

1	baked Ginger Crumb Crust (page 173)
1	1-pound can solid-pack pumpkin puree
½	cup light corn syrup
¾	cup packed light brown sugar
3	large eggs
1½	cups heavy cream or evaporated milk
2	tablespoons dark rum
1	teaspoon vanilla extract
1	tablespoon ground cinnamon
1	tablespoon ground ginger
½	teaspoon freshly grated nutmeg
¼	teaspoon salt

"Cut back on the spices if you're a feeb."

Prepare the baked Ginger Crumb Crust.

Preheat the oven to 350 degrees F, with a rack in the middle. Put the canned pumpkin, corn syrup and brown sugar into the top of a double boiler. Over boiling water, stirring frequently, heat the pumpkin mixture while you prepare the rest of the filling.

In a medium bowl, beat the eggs and stir in the cream or evaporated milk, rum, vanilla extract, spices and salt. Mix well; then stir in the hot pumpkin-sugar mixture. Pour as much of the filling into the baked crust as will comfortably fit. (Bake the rest in 1 or 2 custard cups, as described above.)

Bake for 45 minutes to 1 hour, or until the filling is set. A knife inserted into the center of the pie will come out mostly clean, but bear in mind that the knife cut will show. You can always disguise it with whipped cream if you go this route.

Cool the pie completely and serve it with whipped cream.

Makes one deep 9-inch pie, serving 8.

Orange Buttermilk Sherbet

I GOT THIS RECIPE from a Texas reader named Robert Morrison. Robert recommended using Valencia oranges in the sherbet. I wrote back saying I wasn't sure what Valencias were; would Minneolas work? *He* wrote back: "I don't know what Minneola oranges taste like, though I'm sure your taste and instinct will lead you to a perfectly good substitute. But if you've never tasted a Valencia orange, I think I ought to do something about that. . . . Whether they're from California or Texas, they have a sweeter, fuller flavor than any other oranges I've tried—not in the tangerine direction (I can't bear that piercing, overwhelming smell of tangerines), but more, um, maybe floral or veggie flavored? No, that sounds horrible. I can't describe it, so you'll just have to find out firsthand."

Then he sent me a big huge box of Valencia oranges! When I first saw them, I thought disappointedly, "Oh, he was just talking about plain old *oranges*." That was before I tried them. While plain old juice oranges will work very well—and so will Minneolas, though I have a feeling Robert wouldn't like Minneolas any more than he does tangerines—do use Valencias if you can get them. Whatever you use, though, this is a delicious recipe.

1	tablespoon grated orange rind
1	teaspoon grated lemon rind
1½	cups sugar
1½	cups fresh orange juice
¼	cup fresh lemon juice
2	cups buttermilk, well chilled
1	cup milk, well chilled
1	cup heavy cream, well chilled

In a large bowl, stir the orange and lemon rinds into the sugar. Add the orange and lemon juices to the rind-y sugar, stirring until the sugar dissolves. Add the buttermilk, regular milk and heavy cream. Freeze the mixture in an ice cream maker according to the manufacturer's directions.

Makes about 1½ quarts.

Belgian Buttercake

THIS RECIPE, a Hodgman family staple, came from my mother's friend Diana Lloyd. In the original version, Diana wrote: "People will think you were trying to make shortbread and screwed it up, but they'll come back for more." I myself prefer Belgian buttercake to shortbread; the texture's more interesting.

2   **cups sifted all-purpose flour**
½   **cup plus 2 tablespoons sugar**
¼   **teaspoon salt**
¾   **cup (1½) sticks unsalted butter**
    Milk for painting the top

Preheat the oven to 350 degrees F, with a rack in the middle.

In a medium bowl, stir together the flour, sugar and salt. First cut in the butter with a pastry blender or 2 knives; then gently knead it in with your hands. The dough will be a little crumbly.

Press the dough into the bottom of either a 9-inch pie pan or an 8-inch square pan. Paint the top of the buttercake with a pastry brush dipped in milk.

Bake the buttercake for 25 to 30 minutes, or until it's a pale golden brown. Let it cool for 15 minutes. Cut it into thin wedges if you used the pie pan, or into squares if you used the square pan. Serve at room temperature.

Makes 12 to 16 wedges or about 32 pieces, each 2 x 1 inches.

Hot Chocolate, Iced Tea and Flubber

MY HEART ALWAYS SINKS when I come to the beverage section in a cookbook, just as it sinks when I see a punchbowl at a party. I don't like to think of pineapple bobbing around in a vat of liquid. Not so my sisters, who as children spent hours concocting things like Rainbow Fizzes and Cranberry Tingles from various juices and sherbets. "Garnish with a scoop of lime sherbet" was how their recipes always seemed to end.

My own juice-based drinks have always tended to be simpler. "Swidgle the Jell-O around in your mouth until it liquefies. Spit it back into the spoon and pretend it's medicine. Don't let Mum see." That was probably my earliest contribution to the genre. These days, "Make lemonade" is one I rely on frequently. "Take some juice. Add some seltzer" is another. That's about as far as I go.

But hot chocolate and iced tea—now those are jobs for *scientists*. You could spend your whole life perfecting them.

Although Flubber is semiliquid, no one would call it a beverage—it's inedible—except maybe a child who was much too young to be playing with it in the first place. Like the other recipes here, though, it requires a certain amount of creativity. So I guess these three really do belong together.

Recipes

Hot Chocolate 192

Immaculate Iced Tea 193

Flubber 195

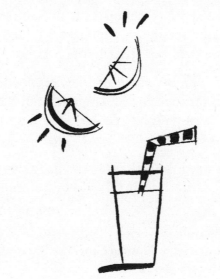

Hot Chocolate

I GOT A VERY NICE LETTER from a reader named John Gregg. "You should have a hot cocoa recipe, definitely," he said. Actually, I drink hot chocolate, not hot cocoa.

For perfect hot chocolate, you need look no farther than that old copy of *My Friend Flicka* in your daughter's room. It's the recipe I once thrust at my father on a hot summer's night when he'd just come in from jogging; I'd reread the book and been seized with a sudden urge to make the hot chocolate Rob and Nell McLaughlin drink after Nell sees the wildcat and gets scared but can't tell Rob about it because he's mad at her for having told one of the hired hands to put the cows in Pasture Sixteen instead of Seventeen, and Nell shouts, "I'll give any orders about the cows I want!" and runs into the house, sobbing with fury. Then, after some other stuff, Rob makes them his special hot chocolate.

"They belted robes about them, went down to the kitchen and Rob made chocolate; for each cup, one square of bitter chocolate and two spoons of sugar and a cup of milk, cooked together until it boiled—a thick, smooth drink, topped with Guernsey cream."

You don't need the Guernsey cream unless you have a Guernsey hanging around Pasture Sixteen. The drink tastes like a delicious hot milkshake.

For Each Cup
- 1 cup milk
- 1 ounce unsweetened chocolate, grated
- 2 tablespoons sugar
- ⅛ teaspoon vanilla extract (optional; I have a feeling Rob wouldn't have thought it was manly)

In a small saucepan over low heat, whisking constantly, heat together the milk, chocolate and sugar until they reach a boil, and the chocolate melts and the sugar dissolves. Stir in the vanilla extract, if using. Serve immediately. It's customary, when making this recipe, to reread all of *Flicka* before you get on with your life.

Makes 1 cup.

Immaculate Iced Tea

I N THE FALL OF 1994, I attended a Harney & Sons Tea Summit in Salisbury, Connecticut. We ate delicious tea-based meals and went to tea seminars and tea tastings and stayed in the White Hart Inn and—but I don't want to make you jealous.

At some point during the weekend, John Harney mentioned that using simple syrup to sweeten iced tea meant you never ended up with sugar in the bottom of your glass. Later, he gave me several more iced tea tips.

Since John used to be an innkeeper, he made iced tea by the gallon. We tend to drink so much of it at my house that a gallon seems like the perfect amount to me, but of course you can cut down the quantity if you'd rather.

It goes without saying that John Harney would prefer you to use Harney & Sons teas. So would I. I'm not just saying that because I went to the Summit, either.

If you want to serve a flavored tea, you're better off *buying* a naturally flavored tea rather than trying to perk it up with your own juices or extracts. "You'll get more intensity that way," John says.

If you're serving iced tea in a punch bowl, and you're making a Bundt-pan-shaped ice ring to put in the bowl, make the ring out of strong tea or lemonade, not water. Why dilute the tea unnecessarily? Any garnish you're floating on top will also look nice frozen inside the ice ring. "Everybody usually uses a slice of lemon, but you can use melon balls and sticks of pineapple, berries. It makes the tea very colorful," John Harney says. Don't overdo it though; you don't want your tea to look too fussy and ladylike.

> "You don't want your tea to look too fussy and ladylike."

Tip One: Start with a tea concentrate. Here's John Harney's method.

10-12	tea bags, any type
1	teaspoon sugar
1	quart boiling water
3	quarts cold water

Place the tea bags in the bottom of a heat-resistant gallon-sized container. (You can also use 4 of Harney & Sons' iced-tea tea bags, each of which makes 1 quart of tea.) Add 1 teaspoon of sugar. "I don't know what the sugar does"—obviously it couldn't actually sweeten that much tea—"but it makes all the difference," John Harney says. Pour 1 quart of boiling water on the tea bags and sugar; let the concentrate steep for a full 15 minutes. Add 3 quarts of cold water, fish out the tea bags and chill the tea until you're ready to serve it.

Makes 1 gallon.

Tip Two: If you sweeten your iced tea, use simple syrup instead of sugar. Here's what you need:

1   **pound sugar**
1   **quart water**

And here's what you do: In a large saucepan, stirring constantly, bring the sugar and water to a boil, dissolving the sugar. Then cool and refrigerate the syrup. That's all. Add the syrup to your tea to taste.

Simple syrup keeps indefinitely in the refrigerator, but be careful that you label the bottle. I once served my friend Alison a big glass of it instead of water. She politely sipped at it without saying anything, thinking I had given her some horrible kind of diet soda.

Tip Three: If your tea turns out cloudy, a tablespoon or so of boiling water will usually clarify it.

Flubber

THIS KIDS' RECIPE is from my friend-and-relation Mimi DiMatteo. Let me quickly say that Flubber is a wonderful molding substance, but it's even *less* edible than most homemade playdoughs. They at least contain salt and flour, whereas Flubber contains glue and Borax. On the other hand, you can't make most homemade playdoughs into weird blobby forms that gradually sink down into themselves as if being obliterated with a slow-action alien melt-gun. What Flubber lacks in plasticity, it makes up for in gross coolness. Also, it's surprisingly easy to clean up.

"I got it from my sister, who got it from a friend," writes Mimi. "I don't think Disney has sanctioned the name, but so what. All you need is Borax, white glue, water, two bowls and a lot of little hands. It's kind of a wet and weird operation, but that's what we like about it."

4	teaspoons Borax
1	cup warm water
	Lots of food coloring
2	cups white glue (craft stores sell really huge bottles if you don't want to buy lots of little ones)
1½	cups very hot water

"Now start playing, but don't eat."

In a small bowl, mix the Borax with the warm water. Stir with fingers to dissolve. Add some food coloring. (You will need to use lots. Flubber seems to *drink* food coloring.)

In a large bowl, pour the glue into the hot water—as hot as you can get it without burning yourself. Stir with your fingers as you add the glue.

Slowly add the contents of the Borax bowl to the glue bowl, mixing with fingers *constantly*. Keep stirring and mixing until the Flubber no longer sticks to the sides of the bowl. Pour off any excess water; there will almost certainly be some.

Now start playing, but DON'T EAT. Store Flubber in an airtight container. It will keep its flubberiness for about 2 weeks.

Makes 1 quart, enough for 2 to 3 kids.

Leftovers

Apple peelers, the universe's most perfect utensil. How is it that I've seen apple-peeler-corer-slicers for so many, many years and never bought one? Oh, my God! They make apple recipes so *easy*! You just stick the apple onto this forky thing and turn a crank, and all of a sudden your apple becomes a trim, compact spiral of coreless, skinless slices. You can prepare a full pie's worth of apples in about five minutes—and very possibly you can get someone else to do it for you, since the peeler is so much fun to use.

I hope I don't sound like someone who's just discovered that wonderful invention called the "phonograph." But I don't know anyone besides myself and my mother who owns one of these gizmos. (I gave my mother one for Christmas.) Don't even think about making another apple pie without trying an apple peeler. You can get them from the Vermont Country Store (P.O. Box 3000, Manchester Center, VT 05255), Williams-Sonoma and many other places.

Baby bibs, uses for. Old terrycloth bibs make great dish towels. I often snap or tie an old bib onto one of my belt loops as I'm cooking. I'm even thinking that I might go out and buy a few new bibs just for this purpose. My old ones are getting awfully ratty, which I guess shouldn't surprise me since my younger child is almost 8 years old now.

Bacon, Carol's. As I've said elsewhere in this book, my mother-in-law Carol Owen is my bacon soulmate. Long ago she figured out a way to partially cook bacon so that you can store it in the freezer and whip it out whenever you want a couple of slices. You can even finish cooking it in the toaster oven if you want. We call this pork product "Grammie bacon."

What Carol does is, she cooks the bacon until it's—as she puts it—"not totally floppy, but not clear." In other words, until about half the fat has been cooked out. Carol then drains the bacon well and freezes it in a single layer on a cookie sheet so that the pieces won't stick together. Once the bacon is frozen, she puts it into a freezer container and uses it as needed. You can finish cooking Grammie bacon in the toaster oven, regular oven or skillet. (I don't recommend the microwave.) It takes only a few minutes, and you won't be left with buckets of bacon grease because you've already *removed* buckets of bacon grease the first time around.

Carol always brings some Grammie bacon to our house when she and my father-in-law come to visit. We think, "Oh, now we'll be able to eat bacon for breakfast for days and days," but then we usually eat most of it within a couple of hours.

By the way, I've discovered that turkey bacon is pretty good. It doesn't taste like true bacon when you eat it plain, but it makes a decent substitute in most recipes as long as you cook it very crisp. In other words, you can use it on your family.

Brown sugar, the easiest way to keep moist. As soon as you've opened a bag of brown sugar, tuck a piece of bread in with the remaining sugar. Seal the bag tightly. Just use regular old store bread; this time, you *want* the preservatives. Homemade bread would get moldy too quickly.

Cocoa, please use the right kind of. I'm not talking about whether to use Dutched or natural cocoa. I'm talking about *please* buy your cocoa from the King Arthur Flour catalog (see page 199 for the King Arthur number). They sell Merckens cocoa, which—like all Merckens products—is much better than what you can buy in ordinary stores. It's twice as rich as store cocoa and is available in both Dutch-process and natural.

Cookbooks, writing in. Think of your cookbooks as textbooks, not library books. You don't have to keep them clean. You're *supposed* to write in them. Just as the most-used recipes will have the most

stains and grease spots on the pages, so they should also be black with written addenda. I make lots of notes in the margins: spice additions, suggestions for spots where the recipe gets difficult, things like "Loyd's favorite." "Bad recipe" is something I also write in cookbooks a lot, or "Doesn't work." I do this because if a recipe is lusciously described, I tend to forget whether I've made it before, and only remember when I taste it again or it can't be removed from the pan again, or whatever went wrong with it before goes wrong again.

D'Artagnan, the marvels of. I swear I'm not a flak for all these catalogs. I just want you to know about them because they're so, so great. D'Artagnan sells "Foie Gras and Game/Fresh and Prepared." I'm not that interested in the foie gras, but the company's meats are wonderful. They sell all-natural products; their meat, game and poultry are hormone-free, and their poultry is free-range. No endangered species, no poached meats, nothing is ever frozen—come *on*, let's *go*! Among other meats, they sell chicken, poussin, several kinds of duck (even boned duck breasts), venison, elk, hare, kid and, and, and. They also sell prepared dishes like cassoulet, confit and venison daube. For a catalog, call 1-800-DARTAGN. Here, let me translate that for you: 1-800-327-8246.

Flour, keeping it fresh. Whenever your canister of flour gets low, do you refill it before it's empty because you like the cozy look of a full canister? Well, stop it. Flour gets rancid just like everything else. If you keep topping it off, nothing will happen for awhile. But then one day you'll find you're completely out of flour and *have* to use the stuff at the bottom of the canister, and that's the day you'll realize how awful stale flour tastes. If you don't like the look of an almost-empty flour container on your counter, move it inside some cupboard where you won't have to look at it.

Another problem with flour is those horrible Indian meal moths that like to set up house in flour-related products. I never saw a meal moth until we moved out of New York; I guess they moved in to occupy the slot that had previously been filled by cockroaches. If your pantry is infested with these icky little guys, there are two things you can do. First, move as many grain products as you can to the freezer or the refrigerator, where the moths can't get at them. I keep cornmeal and oatmeal in the fridge, and all my exotic flours, rices and pastas in the freezer. I also freeze all my birdseed and rabbit food.

Second, buy moth traps from Gardens Alive!, an organic garden-supply company. These traps are lined with a moth-attracting pheromone. Putting five or six into your pantry will help a lot. I know it's not a very nice thing to do to the moths, but I can't work up much sympathy for insects that get into my food. Gardens Alive! has many other cool products: packets of green lacewing eggs, grass that doesn't grow as tall and so doesn't need to be cut as often, humane deer repellent. ("Unless there's no choice but starvation, deer and rabbits will not eat treated plants.") To get the Gardens Alive! catalog, call 1-812-537-8650.

Oh, and another flour thing: Always wash and rinse your hands thoroughly before you open a new bag of flour. Just a trace of perfume or soap on your hands can get onto the edge of the open bag and taint batch after batch of baked goods.

Garlic bulbs, a unique way to show off with. Some gift shops sell ceramic garlic bulbs as placecard holders. I was lustfully staring at a set of these in a catalog when it occurred to me that I could just use *real* garlic cloves as placecard holders if I cut a notch in their sides to stick the cards in. I haven't actually tried this yet, but any day now I probably will. Come to think of it, there's no reason other edibles couldn't be used for the same purpose. Baby artichokes would hold placecards *perfectly*. Tulip bulbs would work too. Now all I have to do is transform myself into the kind of person who uses placecards.

Hazelnuts, blanching. To get those nasty papery skins off your hazelnuts, you should first of all buy the blanched hazelnuts from the King Arthur Flour catalog. (See the next entry for a lengthy rave about this catalog.) But if you need skinned hazelnuts *right now*, these two tips will make it easier. First, before toasting, mist the nuts with water from a plant mister (or just put them in a sieve and briefly run water over them, shaking off all excess). Then, when they're toasted, cool them for a minute, put them into a food processor fitted with the plastic bread blade, and process them until most of the skins have come off. I got this second tip from a King Arthur

Flour handout, which adds, "Some of the nuts will crack, but you'll be amazed how effective and easy this technique is."

The King Arthur Flour Baker's Catalog, about. To think that I never knew about this catalog until my friend Andy Aaron mentioned it a few months ago. What rock was I living under? Everyone else seems to know about it. I can't begin to describe its marvels, so I'll just describe a few of the ways my money has disappeared since my first catalog came in the mail. My kitchen is now graced with:

European Baker's Yeast, a high-performance yeast specially developed for professional bakers—of which I'm not one, but I like to pretend.

Vegalene, a pan spray that's much better than the supermarket kind. (You can also spray it on top of your bread dough to give it "a deep, rich, golden crust.") They sell olive oil in spray form too. I don't like olive oil, but since you probably do, you might want to know about this.

Nonaluminum baking powder—*very, very important*. You must instantly stop using your ordinary baking powder and switch to Mainewell Bakewell Cream Baking Powder, which tastes better (I tried some plain) and makes your baked goods rise higher. There's a rumor that it's healthier too. That's not why I buy Mainewell, since I have a fatalistic feeling that I'm going to catch *all* the diseases, but it's nice to know that for once the better-tasting choice is also healthier.

Pure lemon, lime and orange oils. You can re-place grated rind with these, but I like to use them as an extra citrus touch along with rind and juice.

Pounds and pounds of Merckens' unsweetened chocolate, as different from the grocery-store variety as silk from cement.

Heat-resistant "rubber" spatulas that can handle temperatures from −100 degrees F to 500 degrees F. (They're not actually made of rubber but of some modern miracle material.) If you buy these spatulas, draw a star on the handle with permanent marker so you'll know which ones they are.

A potato ricer that can handle big, huge amounts of potato at one time.

Deep-blue, washable suede potholders that work just as well as the regular kind and look much better. As the catalog put it, these replace those "inexpensive, cheery" potholders. Anyone who uses "cheery" as a negative gets my vote.

I could go on and on, but you see what I mean, don't you?

The King Arthur Flour Baker's Catalog is required bedside reading for every warm-blooded vertebrate. Their number is 1-800-827-6836.

Maid of Scandinavia: gone! In *Beat This!*, I went on and on about Maid of Scandinavia, an unparalleled bakers' and confectioners' supply house. Unfortunately, Maid of Scandinavia has since disappeared. Fortunately, it's been bought by a company called Sweet Celebrations, and most of the inventory is the same. For my husband's birthday, I was able to buy just as many golf-motif cake decorations from

Sweet Celebrations as I could have from Maid of Scandinavia. I also bought a little plastic man humorously grimacing over a charred piece of meat; David likes to barbecue things, you see. Sweet Celebrations' toll-free number is 1-800-328-6722.

Parchment paper, why Laurie Colwin was right when she said that whoever invented it deserved the Nobel Prize. In this cookbook, I haven't told you to use parchment paper—also called baking parchment—nearly as much as I actually use it myself. I usually tell you to butter the pan instead. But I'm only doing that a) so you won't get scared away from the recipe if you don't have any parchment paper in the house and b) so I won't be forcing you to break my rules if you *refuse* to use parchment paper.

Truly, though, parchment paper is worth using for almost any baked good that's baked in a flat pan. Butter the pan; then line it with parchment paper cut to fit. (If you're baking a cake, butter and flour the parchment paper as well.) It only takes a couple of seconds, but it yields *years'* worth of satisfaction.

If you really can't stand the bother of using parchment paper, you might at least invest in a Teflon pan liner from the King Arthur Flour catalog. (See the King Arthur entry, page 199.) These liners are reusable. They make cookie baking way, way easier.

Plastic wrap, another good use for. I only use Saran Wrap, but any plastic wrap will work for this trick. If you're making a heavy dough in an electric mixer or food processor—the kind of dough that makes the machine shake a lot—tuck a crumpled-up piece of plastic wrap under the front of the machine's base. This will help to keep the machine from lurching over the edge of the kitchen counter when you turn your back.

Plastic wrap is a great way to transport fragile baked goods. Crumple it into small balls and tuck them into your container of cake or cookies or whatever. The balls will uncrumple to fill the space, which will keep the contents from shaking around.

Rye flour, worth keeping on hand. I like rye bread fine, but I never used to buy rye flour because I thought it would make all my baked goods taste sour. In fact, a bit of rye flour adds an indefinably sweet and nutty quality to many basic baked goods—pancakes, waffles, muffins, Yorkshire pudding. I always keep a small bag of it in the freezer.

Scissors, more frequent use of. I wish I could write a whole cookbook about scissors. They're so much easier to use than knives! Here are a few things you can do with a good strong pair of stainless-steel kitchen scissors: Cut pizza. Chop up canned tomatoes (and other messy solids) right in the can so you don't have to pour them into a bowl and get red splatter-dots all over your counter. Chop parsley. Cut square biscuits, after you've dipped the scissors in flour. (Scissors won't mash down the dough as much as a knife would.) Cut caramels, after you've buttered the scissor blades. Cut out strips of dough for things like cinnamon sticks and bread sticks and cheese straws. Yes, scissors are a wonderful thing. My friend Patty says I should set the table with scissors at each place.

Scoops, the greatness of. A *Cook's Illustrated* reader, Leo Gallagher, wrote in to suggest loading pastry bags with an ice cream scoop. The King Arthur Flour catalog sells a small muffin scoop for filling—yes!—muffin tins. Both suggestions are invaluable, though the latter isn't really a suggestion. Well, I guess the King Arthur people are "suggesting" that you buy their scoop.

One place I don't use scoops is in my flour and sugar canisters. I keep ½-cup measuring cups in there instead. That way, if I just need a cup or so of flour or sugar, I can get it quickly.

Soap, storing. This isn't a cooking tip, but when else will I ever get to give it to you? If you use bar soap (as opposed to the liquid kind), don't store it on one of those spiky soap-holding things. Instead, store it on a fingernail-cleaning brush. It keeps the soap dry and keeps the nail brush where you can easily find it.

Sticky syrups' bad habit of grossly clogging their jars. As soon as you open a jar of molasses, honey or any other syrup, oil the threads on the jar with a paper towel dipped in corn oil. (By threads, I mean what *I* call the "lid-screw-on part.") This will prevent the horrible sticky-jar-top buildup that sometimes makes me afraid to open molasses jars.

Superfine sugar, my very annoying request that you use. My recipes often call for superfine sugar, but I'm not just doing it to show off. Superfine sugar is simply granulated sugar that's been ground to a finer grade. It's also called "bar" sugar—I guess because it dissolves better in mixed drinks—and can usually be found in the baking section of the supermarket. I buy it in Domino's 1-pound boxes. It dissolves instantly and is well worth keeping on hand. In any recipe that calls for regular granulated sugar, you can substitute an equal amount of superfine.

Using superfine sugar in recipes where the sugar isn't cooked ensures that the final product won't be gritty. Using it in regular baking gives the baked good a finer texture; I don't bother with it for cookies, but I do for cakes. Using it in candy makes it much less likely that the candy will crystallize accidentally.

Superfine sugar isn't the same as powdered or confectioners' sugar, neither of which should ever be substituted for granulated unless you *want* to ruin whatever you're making.

If you can't find superfine sugar and want to try making some, you can process ordinary granulated sugar in the food processor for 5 minutes or so. Make sure to cover the feeder tube with your hand or a bowl, or a cloudy puff of sugar will rise out and descend all over your counter. The resulting sugar won't be nearly as fine as real superfine, but it will be less gritty than regular granulated.

Index

A

Almond Pastry, Mrs. Westerman's, 34
Almond Tart, Ingrid's, 148
Appetizers, 14-30. *See also* Hors d'Oeuvres
Apple
    Cider Syrup, 144
    Crisp, Very Controversial, 150
    peelers, about using, 196
    Pie, Updated, 151
Applesauce, Upgraded, 138
Asparagus Vinaigrette, Cindy's, 107
Avocado. *See* Guacamole

B

baby bibs, about using, 196
bacon, cooking partially, 196
Bacony Split Pea Soup, 67
Bagels, 36; Cinnamon-Raisin, 38
"Barbecued" Pork Loin, Cold, 89
Beans, Baked, 108
Beans, Seven-Layer Dip, 14
Beef
    Flank-Steak, Mustard-Glazed, 79
    Pot Roast with Leeks and Brandy, 91
    The Roast, 92
    Stew, 72

Belgian Buttercake, 189
Biscuits
    Herb, 41; variation (refrigerated dough), 42
    Onion, Cheddar and Chive, 39
    Pumpkin, 43
Blondies, Coffee-Almond, 158
Blueberry Pie, Laura and Emmy's, 155
Bread
    English Muffin, 47
    Garlic, The Greatest, 47
    Soda, 56
Breakfast Foods, 34-58
    Almond Pastry, Mrs. Westerman's, 34
    Bagels, 36; Cinnamon-Raisin, 38
    Biscuits, Onion, Cheddar and Chive, 39
    Coffee Cake, Sour Cream, 44
    Corn Muffins, 49
    Crackers, Plain, 46
    English Muffin Bread, 47
    Garlic Bread, The Greatest, 47
    Herb Biscuits, 41; variation (refrigerated dough), 42
    Oatcakes, 53
    Popovers, 54
    Pumpkin Biscuits, 43
    Seven-Glazed Lemon-Poppy Seed Muffins, 51
    Soda Bread, 56

Waffles, Better Than That Damn Mix, The Only, 58
Brine for Shrimp, 28
Brining Solution for Turkey, 101
brown sugar, keeping moist, 197
Brownies, Coffee-Almond, 158
Brussels Sprouts, The Best, 110
Buttercake, Belgian, 189

C

Cake
    Belgian Buttercake, 189
    Chocolate, Another Drop-Dead, 168
    Hodgecakes, 162
    Mix, Part I, The Best Thing to Do with a, 160
    Mix, Part II, The Best Thing to Do with a, 164
Caramel Sauce, Schrafft's Authentic, 166
Carrot Salad, Gingered, 112
Carrots, Easter, 111
Champagne Risotto, 126
Cheddar, Onion and Chive Biscuits, 39
Cheese
    and Macaroni, Mature, 87
    Soufflé, Do Not Make Any But Lucy Dobson's, 98
    -Stuffed Baked Potatoes, 119

Cherry Tomatoes, Something to Do with, 113
Chicken
    Breasts, Parsley-Parmesan (The Best Use of Boned Chicken Breasts), 76
    Lasagna, Lisa Lasagna's, 84
    Sticky Chicky, 74
    Wedding, 78
Chocolate
    Cake, Another Drop-Dead, 168
    Cake Mix, Part I, 160
    Chip Cookies, Thin, Chewy, Buttery, 170
    Hodgecakes, 162
    Hot, 192
    Pudding, Instant, 172
Chutney
    Cranberry, 139
    Lime, 142
    Posy's, 141
Cinnamon-Raisin Bagels, 38
cocoa, right kind of, 197
Coffee-Almond Brownies, 158; Blondies, 158.
Coffee Cake, Sour Cream, 44
cookbooks, writing in, 197
Cookies
    Chocolate Chip, Thin, Chewy, Buttery, 170
    Coffee-Almond Brownies, 158; Blondies, 158
    Ginger Squares, 175
    Molasses, New, 183
    Oatmeal, Aunt Gail's, 185
Corn Chowder, Roast Garlic, 63

Corn Muffins, 49
Crackers, Plain, 46
Cranberry Chutney, 139
Crocked Shrimp, 16
Crust, Ginger Crumb, 173

D

D'Artagnan catalog (meats), 197
Dessert, 148-89
    Apple Crisp, Very Controversial, 150
    Apple Pie Updated. 151
    Belgian Buttercake, 189
    Blueberry Pie, Laura and Emmy's, 155
    Cake Mix, Part I, The Best Thing to Do with a, 160; Part II, 164
    Caramel Sauce, Schrafft's Authentic, 166
    Chocolate Cake, Another Drop-Dead, 168
    Chocolate Chip Cookies, Thin, Chewy, Buttery, 170
    Chocolate Pudding, Instant, 172
    Coffee-Almond Brownies, 158; Blondies, 158
    Ginger Crumb Crust, 173
    Ginger Squares, 175
    Grapefruit Gelatin, 179
    Hodgecakes, 162
    Key Lime Pie, 180
    Lemon Pies, Frozen, The Last Word in, 182
    Licorice Ice Cream, 177

Molasses Cookies, New, 183
Oatmeal Cookies, Aunt Gail's, 185
Orange Buttermilk Sherbet, 188
Pumpkin Pie, Perfect, 186
Tart, Almond, Ingrid's, 148
Dip, Seven-Layer, 14
Dipping Sauce, Terry's, 20

E

Egg Rolls, Philippine (Lumpia), 18
Egg Salad, The Best (In Memory of Patty Marx), 62
English Muffin Bread, 47

F

Flank-Steak, Mustard-Glazed, 79
flour, keeping it fresh, 197
Flubber (playdough), 195
Frozen Lemon Pies, The Last Word in, 182

G

Garlic
    Bread, The Greatest, 47
    bulbs (and other vegetables) as placecards, 198
    Roast, Corn Chowder, 63
Gelatin, Grapefruit, 179
Ginger
    Crumb Crust, 173
    Honey, 145

Squares, 175
Gingered Carrot Salad, 112
Glaze, Pantry Ham, 80
Granola, God's (Asian Ambrosia, Posy's Cheewrah, St. John's Trail Mix), 21
Grapefruit Gelatin, 179
Green Beans in Tomato Vinaigrette, 114
Guacamole, Many-Splendored, 24
Guacamole, Seven-Layer Dip, 14

H

Ham, Two Things You Have to Serve with:
    Pantry Glaze, 80
    Pantry Mustard, 81
hazelnuts, blanching, 198
Herb Biscuits, 41; variation (refrigerated dough), 42
hints. *See* Leftovers
Hodgecakes, 162
Honey, Ginger, 145
Hors d'Oeuvres, 14-30
    Dipping Sauce, Terry's, 20
    Granola, God's, 21
    Guacamole, Many-Splendored, 24
    Lumpia (Philippine Egg Rolls), 18
    Pepper-Parmesan Cocktail Shortbread, 26
    Seven-Layer Dip, 14
    Shrimp, Crocked, 16
    Shrimp, Party, 28

Smoked Salmon Spirals, 27
Spiced Vanilla Pecans, 25
Tomato Sandwiches, Sarah's, 30
Hot Chocolate, 192

I

Ice Cream. *See also* Sherbet
    Licorice, 177
Iced Peach Soup, 64
Iced Tea, Immaculate, 193

K

Key Lime Pie, 180
The King Arthur Flour Baker's Catalog (baking supplies), 199

L

Lamb, Leg of, Marinated Butterflied, 82
Lasagna, Lisa Lasagna's, 84
Leeks and Brandy, Pot Roast with, 91
Leftovers (hints), 196-201
    apple peelers, about using, 196
    baby bibs, about using, 196
    bacon, cooking partially, 196
    brown sugar, keeping moist, 197
    cocoa, right kind of, 197
    cookbooks, writing in, 197
    D'Artagnan catalog (for meats), 197
    flour, keeping it fresh, 197

garlic bulbs (and other vegetables) as placecards, 198
hazelnuts, blanching, 198
The King Arthur Flour Baker's catalog (baking supplies), 199
Maid of Scandinavia/Sweet Celebrations (baker's supply house), 199
parchment paper, about using, 200
plastic wrap, about using, 200
rye flour, using, 200
scissors, uses for, 200
scoops, uses for, 201
soap, storing, 201
sticky jar tops, preventing, 201
superfine sugar, using, 201
Sweet Celebrations (baker's supply house), 199
Lemon Pies, Frozen, The Last Word in, 182
Lemon-Poppy Seed Muffins, Seven-Glazed, 51
Licorice Ice Cream, 177
Lime Chutney, 142
Lumpia (Philippine Egg Rolls), 18

M

Macaroni and Cheese, Mature, 87
Maid of Scandinavia/Sweet Celebrations (baker's supply house), 199
Main Dishes, 72-101
    Beef Stew, 72

Cheese Soufflé, 98
Chicken Breasts, Parsley-
  Parmesan, 76
Chicken, Sticky Chicky, 74
Chicken, Wedding, 78
Flank Steak, Mustard-Glazed,
  79
Ham, Glaze for, 80; Pantry
  Mustard for, 81
Lamb, Leg of, Marinated
  Butterflied, 82
Lasagna, Lisa Lasagna's, 84
Macaroni and Cheese, Mature,
  87
Pork Loin, Cold "Barbecued,"
  89
Pot Roast with Leeks and
  Brandy, 91
The Roast Beef, 92
Salmon, Perfect, 94
Shrimp with Feta and Fennel,
  96
Tortellini with Pistachio Sauce,
  100
Turkey, Perfected, 101
Marinated Butterflied Leg of
  Lamb, 82
Mashers, CMO's, 123
Millet, Tomato Soup with, 68
Molasses Cookies, New, 183
Muffins, Corn, 49
Muffins, Seven-Glazed Lemon-
  Poppy Seed, 51
Mustard-Glazed Flank Steak, 79
Mustard for Ham, Pantry, 81

O

Oatcakes, 53
Oatmeal Cookies, Aunt Gail's,
  185
Onion, Cheddar and Chive
  Biscuits, 39
Orange Buttermilk Sherbet, 188

P

Pancakes. See Oatcakes
Pantry Ham Glaze, 80
Pantry Mustard, 81
parchment paper, about using,
  200
Parsley-Parmesan Chicken
  Breasts (The Best Use of Boned
  Chicken Breasts), 76
Party Shrimp, 28; Brine for, 28
Pasta
  Lasagna, Lisa Lasagna's, 84
  Macaroni and Cheese, Mature,
    87
  Salad, Springtime, 115
  Tortellini with Pistachio Sauce,
    100
Pastry, Almond, Mrs.
  Westerman's, 34
Peach Soup, Iced, 64
Pecans, Spiced Vanilla, 25
Pepper-Parmesan Cocktail
  Shortbread, 26
Philippine Egg Rolls (Lumpia),
  18
Pie(s)
  Almond Tart, Ingrid's, 148

Apple, Updated, 151
Blueberry, Laura and Emmy's,
  155
Key Lime, 180
Lemon, Frozen, The Last
  Word in, 182
Pumpkin, Perfect, 186
Plain Crackers, 46
plastic wrap, about using, 200
Popovers, 54
Poppy Seed-Lemon Muffins,
  Seven-Glazed, 51
Pork. See also Ham
  Loin, Cold "Barbecued," 89
Pot Roast with Leeks and Brandy,
  91
Potato(es)
  Baked, Cheese-Stuffed, 119
  A Famous Person's, 122
  Mashers, CMO's, 123
  Party, 120
  Salad, Kurt's, 117
Pudding, Instant Chocolate, 172
Pumpkin Biscuits, 43
Pumpkin Pie, Perfect, 186

Q

Québecois Vinaigrette, 134

R

Rice Salad, 124
Risotto, Champagne, 126
The Roast Beef, 92
Roast Garlic Corn Chowder, 63
rye flour, using, 200

S

Salad. *See also* Vinaigrette
    Carrot, Gingered, 112
    Egg, The Best (in memory of Patty Marx), 62
    Hot Polish (cabbage apple), 131
    Layered, Upgraded, 127
    Pasta, Springtime, 115
    Potato, Kurt's, 117
    Rice, 124
    Snow Pea, 129
    Watercress Slaw, 130
Salmon, Perfect, 94
Salmon, Smoked, Spirals, 27
Salsa Soup, 65
Sandwich, Egg Salad, The Best (In Memory of Patty Marx), 62
Sandwiches, Tomato, Sarah's, 30
Sauce, Caramel, Schrafft's Authentic, 166
Sauce, Dipping, Terry's, 20
scissors, many uses for, 200
scoops, uses for, 201
Seven-Glazed Lemon-Poppy Seed Muffins, 51
Seven-Layer Dip, 14
Sherbet, Orange Buttermilk, 188
Sherry Cherry Tomatoes, 113
Shortbread, Pepper-Parmesan Cocktail, 26
Shrimp
    Crocked, 16
    with Feta and Fennel, 96

Lasagna, Lisa Lasagna's, 84
    Party, 28; Brine for, 28
Smoked Salmon Spirals, 27
Snow Pea Salad, 129
soap, storing, 201
Soda Bread, 56
Soufflé, Cheese, Do Not Make Any But Lucy Dobson's, 98
Soup, 63-68
    Peach, Iced, 64
    Roast Garlic Corn Chowder, 63
    Salsa, 65
    Split Pea, Bacony, 67
    Tomato, with Millet, 68
Sour Cream Coffee Cake, 44
Spiced Vanilla Pecans, 25
Split Pea Soup, Bacony, 67
Springtime Pasta Salad, 115
Squash, Worthwhile Winter, 132
Stew, Beef, 72
Sticky Chicky, 74
sticky jar tops, preventing, 201
superfine sugar, about using, 201
Sweet Celebrations\Maid of Scandinavia (baker's supply house), 199
Sweet Potatoes, Jace's Favorite, 133
Syrup, Apple Cider, 144

T

Tart. *See also* Pie
    Almond, Ingrid's, 148

Tea, Iced, Immaculate, 193
Tomato(es)
    Cherry, Something to Do with, 113
    Sandwiches, Sarah's, 30
    Soup with Millet, 68
    Vinaigrette, Green Beans in, 114
Tortellini with Pistachio Sauce, 100
Turkey, Perfected, 101; Brining Solution for, 101

V

Vanilla Pecans, Spiced, 25
Vinaigrette
    Asparagus, Cindy's, 106
    Québecois (dressing), 134
    Tomato, Green Beans in, 114

W

Waffles, Better Than That Damn Mix, The Only, 58
Watercress Slaw, 130
Wedding Chicken, 78
Winter Squash, Worthwhile, 132

Z

Zucchini, No, This Really Is Different! 135

About the Author

ANN HODGMAN started cooking early, and at the age of 14 was named *Seventeen* magazine's Teen Gourmet of the Year. Since then, she has worked as a chocolatier and a caterer. Besides *Beat This! Cookbook*, she is the author of 40 books for children and several humor books for adults and was the original food columnist for *Spy* magazine. She and her husband live in Washington, Connecticut, with their two children, a dog, two cats, a cockatiel, two parakeets, a hedgehog, three rats, two hamsters, two African pygmy mice, three Australian flying squirrels, two prairie dogs, two turtles and a rabbit.